Hamlyn all-colour paperbacks

Plantagenet Somerset Fry

Collecting Inexpensive Antiques

Hamlyn · Londo

FOREWORD

There seem to be so many books about antiques and collecting these days that one hesitates to inflict yet another on a long-suffering public. The principal justification for this one is that, while there is a growing number who enjoy a standard of living which allows them to buy occasional antiques of value, the supply is not rising to meet the demand, and people are now beginning to collect in fields which a decade ago few even considered. They may benefit from a guide which can be bought cheaply and slipped into a pocket for quick reference.

A few years ago I was severely injured in a road accident, and for a time it was doubtful whether I would ever walk properly again. Then a miracle happened. Many people were very good to me during those difficult times. They are never forgotten — nor ever could be — and this book is dedicated to them.

P.S.F.

Published by the Hamlyn Publishing Group Limited
London · New York · Sydney · Toronto
Hamlyn House, Feltham, Middlesex, England
In association with Sun Books Pty Ltd., Melbourne

Copyright © The Hamlyn Publishing Group Limited 1973

ISBN 0 600 31785 4
Phototypeset by Filmtype Services Limited, Scarborough
Colour separations by Schwitter Limited, Zurich
Printed in England by Sir Joseph Causton & Sons Limited

CONTENTS

WHAT IS AN INEXPENSIVE ANTIQUE?

When I decided to write this book, I was going to call it *Collecting Junk*. It was a short and crisp title, and to a large extent it summed up what I wanted to say about accumulating inexpensive items made during the last hundred years or so for the use and enjoyment of previous generations. Then I realized that, since much of what, quite honestly, many would label as junk was in fact being eagerly sought by collectors, this could be an offensive disparagement of their taste. So the book is called *Collecting Inexpensive Antiques*.

Collecting for investment was, until recently, the pastime or business of relatively few. But in the last twenty years or so the momentum has gathered, as more and more people have come to regard antiques as a reliable hedge against the shifting value of money. This has naturally pushed up the prices of those things which are generally accepted as antiques, that is, articles of elegance and function at least 130 years old. The age specification stems from the trade's minority view, formulated at the end of the 1950s, that anything manufactured since 1830 is unacceptable as an antique. It was an attempt to stem the growing tendency among many dealers to market good early Victoriana and call it antique. This rule still holds, which means that only the very earliest Victoriana is now acceptable as antique in the circles which laid down the rule.

These circles, however, are getting smaller as the affluence of people in general increases. More people want to collect for investment, and if they cannot afford 130-year-old antiques they will buy articles produced in more recent times. They are also willing to pay for more unusual things – articles which ten or twenty years ago would have been thrown away or not even noticed. There is a whole new world of collectible items produced from about 1850 right up to the Second World War – and perhaps beyond. It is a wide and complicated field, and this book is intended as a pocket guide through the tangle.

Window of a suburban antique shop offering a wide variety of interesting and inexpensive articles. This is the type of shop where a beginner would almost certainly find something to suit his taste and his pocket

(left) Edwardian occasional table and *(right)* late Victorian walnut tip-top table

FURNITURE

In any book on antiques furniture has the lion's share of the pages. The variety of articles is wider than in any other field, and to many people the word antiques simply means old furniture.

Furniture is always functional; it is not always beautiful or elegant. The secret of the best periods, not only of British but perhaps more especially of European furniture, lay in the successful combination of elegance and function. This quality is not to be expected in the furniture we are discussing, for it is not strictly antique at all, and in most cases the functional aspect was clearly more important. The principal exceptions were of course the fine reproductions of earlier styles.

Much Victorian furniture was large – too big, in most cases, for houses built since the Second World War. This furniture is in great demand, however, not only in Britain but also abroad. American buyers, any dealer will tell you, are purchasing this furniture by the van load. So, too, are the Germans, the French, the Dutch, and the Italians. It is a very interesting trend, since, outside Britain, the best furniture of the eighteenth and early nineteenth centuries was made in precisely those countries which are now importing from Britain. It is also interesting that there have been few signs so far that the reverse process is happening. A few British dealers occasionally show pieces of French provincial furniture of the late eighteenth century or reproductions of the nineteenth century, but there is certainly no evidence of mass-importation of furniture from other countries.

Tables

Probably the first piece of furniture one thinks of is a table. For years I wondered why this was so, until I tried an experiment on several friends. I asked them for the first piece they thought of, and it was almost invariably a table. I then asked whether they had learnt Latin at school, and most of them had. *Mensa*, a table, is the first noun one learns in Latin, or at least it was in our day.

In Victorian times the two principal types of dining table were solid square or rectangular mahogany tables with moulded edges and four fat tapering turned, reeded, or polygonal legs. In some cases, the top was separable so that a leaf could be inserted between the two halves. These huge tables need a large room if they are not to dwarf everything else.

Circular mahogany tip-top dining table, about 100 years old

Consequently, they can be found quite cheaply. Cabinet-makers buy them for the wood, which they use for repair or restoration work. One top will often produce several layers of veneer, each with matching grain. Furniture fakers also buy them. They expose the tops to the elements for several months and then use the wood to forge small Regency or Georgian pieces. Sometimes the pieces are hit with chains to simulate the kind of damage one would expect to find after many years of use. This process is called *distressing*.

Ever since the war I have thought of these enormous tables as very reassuring pieces of furniture. They represent the solidity of our Victorian grandfathers and their apparently stable way of life. During the war I was staying in a London house which had a large Victorian table in the breakfast room. We were in this room one day, when the air-raid siren sounded, followed almost at once by a barrage of anti-aircraft fire. Soon we could hear the terrifying intermittent throb of German bombers. There was no time to go down to the shelter, and we were ordered to get under the table and stay there until the all clear was sounded. It was not very comfortable, but I remember well the sense of security that this table afforded.

Another kind of dining table in wide use was the tip-top variety on a central stalk with a tripod or quadrupod base.

(right) Attractive Victorian walnut occasional table with twist turned stalk
(left) Late Victorian ebonized flap-table

Victorian tables for a variety of different uses

The tops were round, oval, or oval with shaped edges. As a rule, the round ones were in mahogany or rosewood, while the oval and shaped ones were in plain or inlaid walnut. They were large enough to seat four to six people, and the tip-up arrangement was particularly useful in those houses which had no separate dining room.

The price for these tables varies amazingly. I have seen them marked as high as £200, and as low as £20. I have one in my garage, which I cannot get £5 for. Its only defect is that the veneer is blistered. Blistering, by the way, is quite common on these tables if they are kept for a long time in centrally-heated houses without humidifiers.

At the end of the nineteenth century and the beginning of this, furniture makers began to copy the older more rectilinear tables, producing gate-leg tables with short or long flaps, refectory tables in the style of the sixteenth and seventeenth centuries, and their own modifications of Regency tables. From an investment viewpoint, one or two good Edwardian reproductions of Georgian tables, providing they are faithful to the styles and well made, would be worth buying now, as in a generation or so it will be much harder to distinguish them from originals. The Edwardian Hepplewhite- or Sheraton-style tables, on the other hand, are instantly recognizable, and indeed there is no evidence that these were supposed to be faithful copies. The return to the lightness and elegance of the eighteenth century was a natural reaction against the heaviness of Victorian furniture, but on the whole lightness was more dominant than elegance.

Tea was another important occasion in Victorian and Edwardian times; the best silver and porcelain were brought out, cook made special cakes and bread, and fine lace and linen tablecloths and doilies were laid on the table. Afternoon tea, according to recent memoirs of Edwardian days, was the time when married women entertained their lovers; their husbands were not expected to be at home for tea, and they seldom were. The tea-tray would be put on an occasional table or a small gate-legged flap table, known as a Sutherland after the Duchess of Sutherland. These tables were made of plain or ebonized walnut, rosewood, or mahogany. The flaps were square, square with canted corners, oval, or round.

Occasional tables were made in many shapes and sizes: some had octagonal tops on four or eight turned legs with gilt lines; some were square or rectangular on centre stalks, or on four round or square legs. Sometimes the tops were inlaid with foliage patterns, festoons of flowers, or even chessboard designs.

Many other kinds of table were used by our grandparents, including card tables with fiddle-pattern tops, envelope tables with four triangular flaps which folded inwards to form the square top above a baize- or leather-lined surface, and work-tables of various designs. Basically, work tables consisted of a hinged top and a hollow conical stem (which provided storage space for silks and cottons), supported either by four legs, or by a tripod or quadrupod base. The tops were sometimes inlaid, and they could be round, square, rectangular, or polygonal in shape. I once had a round chessboard-pattern work-table of about 1890 in my Chelsea shop. Marked at £7 in 1959, I could not sell it. Today I suppose it would cost at least £30.

Late 19th-century display cabinet of oak inlaid with various light woods and mother-of-pearl

Sideboards, dressers, and cabinets

Turning from tables, let us look at sideboards, dressers, and cabinets. Heavy Victorian sideboards were until recent years almost impossible to sell. They were often vast and ugly, and occupied far too much space. Even now the really huge and over-decorated ones are quite inexpensive. The smaller ones, which were often plainer, are more useful and fit quite well into the average sized dining room. For this reason, they are not so cheap, and you may have to spend thirty pounds or so for one in good condition.

Dressers have been made for centuries, and the Welsh dresser is particularly famous. Even those of the nineteenth century are very dear, and are not within the scope of this book. If you want an inexpensive dresser, I can only suggest you look out for a small pine one, which will have been stripped of the paint applied at the time of manufacture. These stripped

Huge Victorian wardrobe with carved ornamentation, and drawers behind the centre mirror

pine dressers are often marked up as antique, even eighteenth century, but they are not as a rule so old; country craftsmen were making them as late as the 1900s, and of course they are being reproduced today.

In Victorian times dressers were used for displaying and storing tableware. They were usually found in the kitchen or scullery. For more decorative pieces of china or glass, display cabinets were used. These stood in alcoves or were placed along the wall between windows. Typical late Victorian and Edwardian cabinets were rectangular and had latticed glass doors, glazed side panels, and four square tapering legs, sometimes with a gallery near the feet. The woodwork was inlaid or painted in the Sheraton manner, and the top was surmounted by a shaped back piece. The shelves were often lined with velvet, and the back panel was either similarly lined or glazed and silvered. There are many of these cabinets to be found today and they are quite cheap. They seem top heavy, and their unsteadiness needs to be watched. If you are going to use one, put the heavier ornaments at the bottom.

Another piece akin to the sideboard was the chiffonier. This was a low cupboard with a marble top surmounted at the back by an ornate, shaped looking-glass. Victorian in design, they were still being produced during the Edwardian period. They had a pair of panelled or silvered glass doors, or, if they were serpentine fronted, there would be a central door and two shaped side doors or just shaped side-shelves. Not long ago you could not give chiffoniers away; now they can cost £25 or more. Those made of mahogany are a little scarcer than those of walnut.

Chests

Many of the chests of drawers made in Victorian and Edwardian times are huge and hideous. Nevertheless, they are extremely useful for storage, and can still be picked up very cheaply. They have either square or bow fronts, sometimes with corner pilasters or bun, turned, or ogee bracket feet. Some have fronts of deal with mahogany veneer, but with deal sides; others are of solid mahogany, oak, satinwood, or rosewood. They usually have big wooden knobs and brass or ivory keyholes, and the drawers, apart from the facing, are of pine or deal.

Victorian dressing table with swivel mirror. Many of the surfaces of this piece are walnut veneered

Smaller chests are much sought after these days and tend to be expensive. A cheaper variation might be a pine chest. Pine chests were originally painted, but now they are being stripped, waxed, and fitted with brass loop handles so that they appear to be Regency or William IV, though in all probability they are no more than a hundred years old.

Towards the end of the nineteenth century, some furniture makers were producing pieces that I would describe as hotel furniture. I do not suppose they were originally intended as such, but they have subsequently appeared in hotels and guesthouses all over the country. This is probably because they could be bought cheaply second-hand. An example of this type of furniture is the chest of drawers with square tapering legs, a rectangular front, and two small drawers at the back on each side of a looking glass pivoted between two pillars. The front of the drawers was inlaid with boxwood, and the handles were brass rings. Another 'hotel' piece was a simpler two-drawered side table with square or turned legs, and a raised gallery on the sides and back.

Chairs

Apart from the more obvious sedentary pursuits, such as eating, relaxing, or studying, chairs have been designed for many other uses and activities. There were, for example, hall chairs, which, in fact, were seldom sat on at all because they had hard seats and hard well-carved backs, sometimes embellished with a coat of arms. There were also plain or upholstered nursery chairs, which had tall vertical backs to make children sit up straight. There were prie-dieus – these were rather like kneelers, but had an upholstered top rail on which

(left) Edwardian armchair vaguely in the French style and *(right)* late 19th-century mahogany bergère chair with cane back and sides

to rest one's arms when praying – and there were squat sewing chairs with broad seats and gently curving backs, which made them very comfortable.

Many of these chairs can still be found for a few pounds, though they will probably need some attention to the upholstery or covers and even to the woodwork.

I was on my way home one day a few months ago, when I saw an antique shop window full of stripped pine furniture. I was looking for a cheap pine bookcase and, as there was one in the window, I stopped to ask the price, only to find that it was ridiculously expensive. Just as I was about to leave I spotted two rather battered nursery chairs, which the dealer was prepared to let me have for £15.

I bought them, put them in the car, and drove off homewards. On the way I called on a dealer friend to see whether he had a bookcase. He had not, but he noticed the chairs in the back of

Two Victorian dining chairs, a hall chair *(right at back)*, c. 1850, and Victorian upholstered nursery chair *(left)*, c. 1850

(left) Edwardian corner chair with inlaid back, and *(right)* Victorian rocking chair of mahogany

the car. After a closer look at them, he bought them from me for £17.50, and so in less than an hour I had made a profit of £2.50! The point is that you can still get chairs of this kind for less than £10 each.

On the other hand, larger chairs of the same shape, with arms, wooden surrounds, button backs, and cabriole legs, are now very expensive. Sometimes the surrounds are padded, so that the whole chair is upholstered, and I have seen this type of chair priced at £100, which is really extortionate.

Among upright chairs, there are still bargains to be found. Many chairs of the latter nineteenth century had balloon backs, that is, the oval backs were shaped to fit the sitter's back. When I had my shop, a set of four in good condition cost about £10. Now, a similar set would cost about £60, and you would probably have to pay £100 for a set of six. Odd chairs, however, can be bought for £6 or £7. A harlequin set of six with similar seats but different backs would be both unusual and attractive. Most chairs of this type were the same height and had seats of the same width. The variations were in the carving on the top and centre rail (if there was one) of the back.

Three typical late Victorian chairs: (*right to left*) balloon-back dining chair, bentwood armchair with cane seat, elmwood kitchen chair

If you dislike rounded chairs, like balloon backs, try the lighter weight Edwardian Sheraton-style. These were squarish chairs with straight backs, cane or lightly upholstered seats, and square or turned tapering legs. They were French-polished, ebonized, or painted. Odd chairs can be found for a pound or so in the rougher types of junk shop. They are really bedroom or parlour chairs, and are not suitable for heavy people to sit on.

A variation of the Edwardian Sheraton chair was the corner chair. The padded seat was roughly triangular in shape, with the apex at the front. The back and sides were formed by carved and decorated panels surmounted by a curved rail, which was supported at the sides by pillar-like upward extensions of the two front legs.

Rocking chairs, although usually not quite so elegant, are extremely comfortable. Some were made in mahogany and thickly cushioned. Others, in mahogany or walnut, had a separate base, which was connected by levers and springs. Bentwood was also used. The use of this material was introduced in Austria in the mid nineteenth century and was an immediate success. It consisted of round strips of beech, which were steamed and bent into shape. The free curving lines, uninterrupted by conventional joints, were then, and would be now, regarded as revolutionary. Ordinary armchairs and upright chairs were also made in bentwood, and you will surely have been to some public hall where row upon row of bentwood chairs with perforated plywood seats line the walls.

Another popular and comfortable chair was the bergère chair, a winged armchair, whose sides, back, and seat were caned between the wooden members. The areas of cane were usually covered by thick cushions or padded on the inside. The arms were often exceptionally low, being no more than a few inches above the level of the seat. The design was introduced by the French in the eighteenth century, when, of course, some exquisite examples were made.

(left to right) Edwardian inlaid nursery chair, upright chair with cane seat, child's bentwood rocking chair

More typical Victorian and Edwardian chairs, together with an elegant two-seater settee

Sofas and settees

Before leaving seats, a word should be said about settees and sofas. There is a difference. Originally, settees were basically three chairs joined together to seat two or three people, and they were usually not luxuriously upholstered. Sofas were settees designed more with comfort in mind, and so that one could recline.

The typical late nineteenth-century sofa had a well-padded curving wooden frame, and cabriole or turned legs. The backs were buttoned, and high at each end; sometimes one end was higher than the other. A variation of this was the day bed, or chaise longue, which had a scroll end raised above the level of the seat. There were also copies of earlier styles, including Regency, William and Mary, and even Elizabethan, with heavy carved oak frames and generous padding. Nineteenth-century sofas were often very large, and, as a general rule, the larger they are the cheaper they are to buy now, but of course you need a generous sized room. Another sofa I have seen is a Morris design, which looks like a double size high wing chair. A sofa of this kind would cost £25 or so.

In the early seventeenth century the owner of Knole House in Kent ordered a couch of a design which, although probably new in England, had been popular in Europe for some time. This was a wide sofa with plush seats and cushions, a high upright, equally soft back, decorated corner posts, and padded arms. Hinged to the top of the arms were upholstered panels, which, when upright, were the same height as the back, but which could be let down on ratchets to provide headrests. Known as the Knole sofa, this design has been imitated frequently, especially at the end of the nineteenth century and the beginning of this.

Apart from tables, chairs, and chests, the Victorians and Edwardians produced many other articles of household furniture, such as bookcases, music cabinets, and corner cupboards, which can still be of practical as well as of decorative value.

The nineteenth-century music cabinet was a tallish narrow walnut cupboard. It had a door, which was either glazed, or panelled with silk or muslin, and inside were six or seven shelves, which were spaced at different intervals. In some

20th-century roll-top desk. These can be found quite cheaply

(left) Late Victorian walnut music cabinet and *(right)* Edwardian envelope games table in mahogany

cases the shelves were edged with strips of red leather, each with a different label, such as *Concertos* or *Sonatas*, tooled in gold. On some cabinets the woodwork was inlaid, and on some the top was surmounted by a three-sided pierced brass gallery. I have seen music cabinets priced at less than thirty pounds. They are very useful – if not for music, for filing papers.

In the nineteenth century corner cupboards were made in mahogany, oak, deal, and pine. Some had open shelves; others had one or two doors, which were either flat or curved. The doors were glazed and latticed, veneered, or painted, and some corner cupboards stood on a lower cupboard with similar doors. The shelves inside were flat-, round-, or serpentine-fronted, but the shape of the front is not necessarily an indication of the value of the piece. Oak corner cupboards with plain panelled doors can be found for fifteen pounds or so. Those with glazed doors make useful display cabinets for porcelain or brass ornaments.

The Victorians and Edwardians loved books, and were generally more avid readers than we are today. The designs of the bookcases and shelves were many and various, from huge shelves in plain mahogany or oak to smaller cases of the kind that had shaped shelves secured by long pegs which protruded through the sides of the case. An innovation of the Edwardian era was the revolving bookcase. This type of bookcase had four sides, each with a book compartment, which was enclosed on one side by a vertical row of slats.

Introduced in the twentieth century was the Globe-Wernicke set of shelves. This consisted of glass-fronted cases, which stacked one on top of the other. Each case was about 12 inches high and housed one row of books. The front could be lifted up and slid into the case along horizontal grooves at the top. These bookcases are more or less dustproof, and can be found

Three pieces made about the turn of the century: *(right to left)* revolving bookshelves, bookcase, Edwardian fall-front bureau with cabriole legs

Ornate Victorian walnut whatnot. Pieces of this kind have become quite expensive in recent years

today for about three pounds a case. They are extremely useful and are bound to appreciate in value.

Fall-front bureaux, with pigeon holes and four long – or two short and three long – drawers in the lower part, have been popular since the latter part of the seventeenth century. Basically, the design has not altered. At the end of the nineteenth century furniture makers were producing bureaux in mahogany, oak, or, more rarely, walnut. Although they were poor imitations, they were quite serviceable. They had bracket or bun feet, or shortish cabriole legs. Pedestal desks, that is, the type with a flat top, and drawers on each side of a central knee-hole, were made in mahogany, oak, walnut, and satin-wood. Some had white porcelain knobs; others were fitted with brass drop or loop handles. The top usually had a leather covering with tooled edges. Surprisingly, this type of desk, which is so useful in many respects, is easy to find. The smaller shiny mahogany ones with porcelain knobs are more expensive, but I know of an oak desk, heavily carved on the top edges and drawers, which for years has been priced at £15 but has not yet been sold.

Gentlemen used long mirrors which were affixed to their wardrobes, either on the outside or on the inside of the doors. They also had cheval looking-glasses. These were long mirrors which were pivoted between two pillars rising from a base of four splayed feet. Some of the late Georgian examples are very elegant. The style was copied in the nineteenth century, and cheaper and uglier mirrors, sometimes with heavy moulding, were produced in mahogany and walnut. The ladies' companion to this was the small toilet mirror, a miniature cheval

Late mahogany washstand, complete with toilet set

(right to left) Small mahogany commode, Victorian ladies' toilet mirror, oak cheval mirror

glass, and these can still be picked up for small sums. The cheapest toilet mirrors are plain and square, while the more expensive types are round or oval and have more elaborate stands.

Bamboo furniture

Towards the end of the nineteenth century, there was a revival of the taste for bamboo furniture, which had been popular in Regency days. The difference was that, while in Regency days the 'bamboo' legs and other members were generally simulated, that is, the wood was turned and notched, and then painted to look like bamboo, the later pieces were actually made of bamboo. Bamboo frames enclosed wickerwork-covered wood panels. Numerous articles were produced, looking, as one commentator has said, rather more fragile than they really were.

The sort of pieces you find today, in many cases standing on the pavement outside an antique or junk shop, are hatstands, shelves, small tables, chests of drawers, often surmounted by a mirror and a complex of small drawers, and overmantels liberally supplied with mirrors. Jüri Gabriel's *Victoriana* (Hamlyn all-colour paperbacks) has a picture of a mid-Victorian writing desk with bamboo legs, but this is an unusual piece.

Ten years ago you would probably not have given this kind of furniture much thought, and it does not seem to have been collected on any scale. It was, however, almost mass-produced by several London firms. In a way, it was symbolic of the British Empire. Middle-class people felt comforted using furniture which they believed came from some oriental outpost coloured pink on the map. Some may even have been smug

Three pieces of bamboo furniture: *(right to left)* corner whatnot with mirrors at the top, occasional table with lacquered wood top, writing table

enough to imagine they were doing the natives a favour by patronizing their craft industries.

In recent years there has been a sudden increase in the demand for bamboo furniture, especially among American buyers. As a result, it is no longer cheap. I had to pay thirty pounds for a bedroom suite comprising a wardrobe, chest of drawers, washstand, and upright chair, which were all in indifferent condition. Bamboo furniture is not unattractive, and a bedroom furnished with it would certainly surprise your friends. Repairs, however, could present a problem, for there do not seem to be many restorers either expert or interested in such work.

Oak reproductions

There is one more category of furniture which is still relatively inexpensive, and that is the late Victorian and Edwardian oak reproductions of sixteenth-, seventeenth-, and eighteenth-century designs. This furniture is immediately recognizable; it is almost always heavy, very dark, poorly carved, badly proportioned, and over decorated. Typical pieces include

Reproduction of 17th-century oak court cupboard, c. 1910

(right) Reproduction oak coffer with linenfold decoration, and
(left) late Victorian idea of an oak settle

buffets, sideboards, bookcases, corner cupboards, and settles.

These reproductions are quite distinct from the fine Tudor and Gothic reproductions which were being produced by the Warwickshire school of craftsmen from about 1850. The coarser oak is marked by a roundness on many edges and surfaces which you would expect to be sharp. This was as a result of using machines rather than hand tools. Mouldings, carvings, and other features tended to lack character, and the carvings were often out of style. A pedestal desk, for example, which was more or less Georgian in its proportions and design, would have rococo or possibly Art Nouveau motifs on the drawers.

Despite its coarseness, I would not turn my nose up at this type of furniture, for in a large well-proportioned room where it will not swamp everything else it can be supremely functional. A huge double bookcase, for example, with shiny varnish on the dark oak will look far less overpowering if you paint it white, and some people pick out the carved areas in different colours. I would suggest using emulsion paint, however, as it may be easier to scrape off, should you later decide to revert to the natural wood colour.

Various mantel clocks, a ship's clock *(far right)*, and an English dial clock *(left at back)*, once a common feature of schoolrooms

CLOCKS AND WATCHES

One hundred and fifty years ago only the wealthy had clocks. Then, as the standard of living began to improve for a wide range of people in Europe and America, more people were able to afford a clock, and makers began to produce simpler and cheaper designs.

Among the earliest clocks produced in some quantity were those the Victorians dubbed grandfather clocks. More properly known as longcase clocks, they had been invented in the seventeenth century and after about 1750 began to be made in considerable numbers. As may be expected, however, the general quality and fineness of finish deteriorated. The earlier brass or silver dials, which were not more than about 10 inches in diameter, gradually gave way to bigger dials, 12 inches or more across and made of painted metal or wood. During the nineteenth century the more elegant Georgian designs of hoods and cases became coarser and heavier; some had exaggerated scroll motif decoration or huge, rather ugly pediments. Many clocks of this kind were made and they can be found today for anything from thirty pounds.

Other clocks which are still quite easy to find are the monumental types in poor quality ormulu. They had china faces and were sometimes on wooden plinths. The heavy marble mantelpiece clock that looks a bit like Marble Arch, with its dial in the centre, is considered hideous by many people and accordingly sells very cheaply. I know a dealer who specializes in wooden-cased clocks of the latter nineteenth century. These clocks have fine white porcelain or enamel faces with black Roman or Arabic numerals, and below the dial is a small, shaped extension.

The first mass-produced clocks appeared about 150 years ago. They were shelf clocks, made in the United States for export to Britain and Europe. Generally of rather inferior quality, they often had working parts of wood. They looked like the doors of a church or cathedral, with steeples on each side. The dial was in the upper half, between the sloping sides of the arch, and underneath was a picture or decorated panel. Up to a year or two ago, they could be bought for 50p or even less, and can still be obtained for under £5.

Two typical mid Victorian marble mantel clocks. In the centre a brass and gilt year clock under a dome

Selection of typical Victorian and Edwardian watches

Watches have been made for nearly 500 years. At first, they were not small and slim, but were in fact portable clocks. Their development was slow. Until the invention in 1675 of the spiral balance-spring by Huyghens, who twenty years earlier had introduced the pendulum clock, they were not very accurate, and it was another century before they became small enough to fit comfortably in a pocket.

By the beginning of the nineteenth century, manufacturers in Britain, France, and Switzerland were producing a wide range of watches, usually on chains and in ornate gold or silver cases. Among the cheaper watches were hunters, which had a glass cover over the face and another over the works at the back. There were also half-hunters, whose front cover was gold or silver with a small glazed centre hole to show the position of the hands. Many of these, particularly the silver ones, have survived, and those of the late nineteenth and early twentieth century can be bought for a pound or two, though they usually require some attention.

At night Victorians usually hung their watches on special stands. Watch holders were made of many materials, including wood, china, metal, and bone, and some were of such an elaborate design that the watch itself was almost lost. The Staffordshire factories made a variety of holders in bright colours and odd shapes. A development of these was the larger stand which had a recess for a small clock with a watchlike face. They might be in the form of castle gatehouses, with a recess above the gateway, or of milkmaids with one arm bent to form the recess.

Wristwatches were not invented until towards the end of the nineteenth century, and ladies carried their watches on light chains or suspended from attractive brooches, often in the shape of tied ribbons or love knots.

Any collection of old watches should include some of the early mass-produced ones by Robert Ingersoll, an American industrialist, who in 1892 introduced the Ingersoll one-dollar watch (said to have been 'the watch that made the dollar famous'). Ingersolls were extremely popular in the 1920s and '30s, but by that time the firm was part of the Waterbury Clock Company.

Gold and silver watches, and in the centre an unusual watch stand

(left to right) Indian soapstone figure, Art Nouveau tile, 18th-century
transfer-printed coffeepot, George V coronation beaker

CHINA

In this book the term china is used loosely to mean articles of
porcelain and pottery, although china is more correctly used
only for porcelain and its equivalents. China offers a vast field
for collecting, which is still cheap in many instances and
always fascinating because of the almost limitless scope of
design and colour.

There were many potteries in Britain in the eighteenth
century, including such famous names as Wedgwood, Derby,
Staffordshire (a loose term to cover a number in the county),
Chelsea, and Worcester, but by 1850 there were several
hundred firms producing an enormous amount of ware, either
in sets, both large (some contained over a hundred pieces) and
small, or as individual articles. Over the years many of the huge
sets have been broken up, and odd plates, cups, saucers,

tureens, and dishes can now be found in shops and sales. In many respects the enormous production runs did not result in poor-quality ware, and the oddments, which can still be picked up quite cheaply, are often very fine.

Green-glaze ware – earthenware in the form of leaves and fruits glazed in clear green – was made in England as early as Elizabeth I's reign but was first popularized, after about 1760, by Wedgwood. He produced a variety of articles, such as teapots, plates, and sauce boats, which are now very valuable. During the nineteenth century many potters copied this work, and it has been produced ever since. The easiest articles to find are dessert plates. Many have leaf patterns which occupy the whole surface; sometimes the plate is actually shaped like a leaf. In the late 1950s, when I had my shop, I bought many of these plates and turned them over quite quickly, as long as I did not pay more than five shillings a plate or ask more than six. Once, I was rather rash and bought three at ten shillings

Late 19th-century black-glaze teapot and a selection of cheaper plates. Note the green-glaze leaf pattern plate on the left

each. I still have them. No one has yet offered me a profit! I would not hesitate to recommend collecting green-glaze plates now, while they can still be bought so cheaply.

While on the subject of coloured glaze, another line which can be bought cheaply is shiny black-glaze ware. First produced in the late eighteenth century at Burslem and other places in Staffordshire – articles of this period are valuable – it was widely copied in the mid nineteenth century. Today you can get a black-glaze teapot shaped like a Georgian pot and decorated with gold leaves for under three pounds.

Developing the green-glaze plate theme, do you like decorative plates in general? There is hardly a junk shop which cannot offer you a choice of plates stamped with the mark of a well-known pottery. Many may be only sixty or seventy years old and reproductions of earlier designs produced by the potteries' founders. Look out for rose-patterned Derby porcelain plates, or Worcester plates with plain white centres surrounded by blue and gold edging. Some potters made plates specifically for wall decoration. These often had lacelike rims, through which a piece of ribbon or cord could be threaded to hang them by.

Commemorative china is becoming an increasingly popular

19th- and 20th-century commemorative ware

Collection of Goss ware. The font and busts are unusual pieces

collectors' field. Almost anything was commemorated by our grandfathers, and in all sorts of materials. Beakers, cups, and jugs celebrating the coronation of George V in 1911, or of George VI in 1937 are plentiful, but you will have difficulty in finding commemorative ware for the coronation of Edward VIII. He was never crowned, but he left his abdication so late that one or two firms had already made commemorative plates, cups and saucers, and these have become collectors' pieces.

One Victorian potter who made a substantial contribution to commemorative ware was W. H. Goss of Stoke-on-Trent. He began making articles of very thin moulded porcelain, which was particularly translucent. He made ornaments rather than functional items, and in the earlier years of his business, from about 1860 to about 1890, he produced fine, beautifully coloured ware, including vases, jewellery, and dressing-table articles. Then, not long after Queen Victoria's Golden Jubilee of 1887, he branched out into much cheaper souvenir ware, mainly in the form known as statuary. These articles were shaped like Cleopatra's Needle, Marble Arch,

Nelson's Column, or more mundane things, such as wheelbarrows, cottages, and animals, and decorated with the coats of arms of various towns or resorts. They were produced in huge numbers.

Last one in puts the light out is the caption under a china model of two people getting into bed. This is just one of a variety of figures sold at stalls in travelling fairs towards the end of the nineteenth century. They are called fairings and were imported into Britain from Germany and other European countries. In recent years they have become a very popular collectors' item. Although many of them are now £50 or more, cheaper ones can still be found.

Perhaps the most famous pottery figures of the last hundred years or so are the Staffordshire flatbacks. The Staffordshire potteries produced a vast range of coloured and glazed earthenware figures. They are called flatbacks because only the front view of the figure was properly shaped and coloured. The range included pairs of famous people, such as Queen Victoria and Prince Albert, or Bonnie Prince Charlie and Flora McDonald, which were made either as separate pieces or as pairs on one stand. Sometimes the characters were mounted,

19th-century pinboxes made in Staffordshire and Germany

Some examples of Staffordshire flatbacks. *The Soldier's Return* is second from left

like Lord Raglan and Marshal Arnaud. There were also representations of *The Soldier's Farewell* and *The Soldier's Return*, and there were many portrayals of dogs, especially King Charles spaniels, greyhounds, pugs, and Pekingese.

These Staffordshire figures were made right up to 1900 or so. They fetch high prices in some quarters if the details are good or if it is known that only a limited number was made, but they were usually produced in vast quantities, and careful searching will produce bargains.

When I had my shop I used to buy soapstone figures. Soapstone is a soft, easily carved stone, which comes in many shades of khaki. It was often used for models of rustic scenes, and there were also animal or human representations. One popular figure was of the three wise monkeys. At one time you could not give these away. Now they are being collected and will soon be highly priced.

GLASS

Glass is used both for decorative and functional objects. It looks its best when it gleams in the sunlight. It has proved useful for a long time for vases, wineglasses, bowls for fruit or flowers, smaller bowls for sugar, jam, or marmalade, decanters, jugs for water or cream, tumblers, and tankards, and it has been produced in clear, coloured, and opaque forms.

Articles of glass were generally produced by one of two main processes: blowing or pressing. Blown glass was either free blown, that is, the glass was blown and manipulated into shape by means of hand tools, or mould blown, that is, blown into moulds. Pressed glass was first produced in America in the 1820s. It was made by forcing molten glass into patterned moulds by mechanical means, and could be made to look like better quality mould-blown glass. The Americans produced the best pressed glass for a generation, and it was not until after the Great Exhibition in 1851 that British manufacturers succeeded in ironing out the technical difficulties. Thereafter, pressed-glass articles in a multitude of patterns emerged, and

Some articles from Nailsea: *(left to right)* carafe and tumbler, hat, cider jug

Collection of ruby glass. The cornucopia was used for flower arrangements

it is with these that the collector should begin.

Nailsea

Coloured glass is obviously an attractive ware to collect. It is made by adding metal oxides to the glass mix before blowing or pressing. The glassworks at Nailsea, near Bristol, produced coloured glass of many kinds. Nailsea ware was decorative rather than useful, although a great many jugs, beakers, and bottles were made. One of the typical patterns consisted of a clear background of green or red, with white opaque streaks or coloured threads. The firm began to make this at the end of the eighteenth century, and production was increased once the tax on glass was removed in 1845.

Nailsea – and its many imitators – manufactured a variety of articles known as friggers. These were decorative and sometimes amusing but generally useless items, such as walking sticks, hats, scent bottles shaped like rolling pins, pipes, swords, and shoes. This kind of glass was made right through the nineteenth century, and it is not easy to tell its exact age.

Victorian decanters in cut and pressed glass, tumbler and jug.
The ornate decanter *(left at back)* is Venetian

Ruby glass

Another type of coloured glass that has been collected widely
is the clear red or pink glassware, generally known in this
country as ruby glass and in the United States as cranberry
glass. While it was made for decorative purposes, many functional pieces, such as wineglasses and jugs, were manufactured.
The concentration of colour varied greatly between pink and
carmine, and in building up a set of wineglasses, for example,
it would be difficult to find even six that matched exactly.
If you like ruby glass, however, this will not matter. It was
exceptionally popular in the last decades of the nineteenth
century, and an enormous range of articles was made, including cornucopias for holding flowers, sugar sifters, bowls, and
vases, which were sometimes decorated with pinched colour-
less twists on the outside. There is still so much about that it is
an obvious field for the beginner who is not yet ready to get
his fingers burnt.

Jugs

Among the articles made of better-quality glass in the latter years of the nineteenth century were decanters, claret jugs, and water jugs, and over the years these varied in shape to suit the fashion of the time. Following the introduction by Henry Richardson of a new acid process, which was very similar to that used for engraving copper, many jugs were most beautifully etched with detailed pictures of hunting, pastoral, and garden scenes. The handles were usually gently curved, with reeded moulding to provide a better grip. Such jugs are not cheap now, and you would be lucky to find one under ten pounds. Among the jugs produced in plainer glass were some which had a silver rim, handle, and hinged lid. This type of jug may be Art Nouveau in style (see below), and if you see one with a typical sinuous design buy it.

(left to right) Art Nouveau claret jug with silver-plate fittings, pressed glass water jug, oil lamp with opaline glass shade, Art Deco scent spray

Pub glass

Many other articles in glass are collectible. So far we have looked at small articles, but there are, of course, larger items, such as those wonderful looking-glasses with heavy etching round the edges that one sometimes sees in old pubs which have not been vandalized by modern decorative enthusiasts. Frosted partition screens with trade names or brewing house insignia etched in the centre can sometimes be rescued from pubs which are undergoing modernization, and a few pounds to the foreman will probably secure one. They make interesting wall decoration at home.

Glass chandeliers are another possibility. Of course many are expensive, if only because of the sheer volume of glass, which may be of the crystal variety, but I have seen ornate late Victorian examples go for a few pounds in country sales, largely because few people have a suitable room in which to hang them. Lampshades are also collectible and offer a wide variety of shapes and colours. Although designed for an oil lamp, the tulip-shaped shade with a coloured rim on a white frosted globe can be adapted to fit a modern lamp and will look very attractive.

(below) Victorian pub front with panes of etched frosted glass, and *(right)* mirrors decorated with brewers' insignia and other designs

Paperweights

Until comparatively recently – it has been said that King Farouk of Egypt elevated them to the status of antiques – glass paperweights were inexpensive. Millefiori paperweights were first made in Venice, but the technique was perfected in France during the 1840s, notably by three makers: St Louis, Clichy, and Baccarat. They are heavy domes of clear glass, enclosing canes of coloured glass, which are arranged to look

Group of inexpensive paperweights, including millefiori *(centre front)* and scenic types *(right front)*

like flowers or fruit. Some of the early French ones were wonderfully designed and they now fetch anything up to £8,000 or so, but the poorer and far less well-made ones manufactured in Stourbridge, Bristol, London, or various towns in America can be found at more modest prices. There were also cheaper and much simpler paperweights, many of which were made as souvenirs. You could get plain glass domes or flat blocks, with a picture of, for example, the Colosseum in Rome, the front at Brighton, or a copy of an old county map attached underneath. The picture would be backed by a piece of leather or baize. These scenic paperweights would make a fine collection.

Scent bottles

In Victorian days scent bottles were often made of pressed glass, with silver or silver-plate rims and cut glass or imitation cut glass stoppers. Generally, you bought the bottle empty and had it filled by a chemist or perfumier. The variety of shapes was enormous. The larger scent bottles were made in the shape of flagons or decanters.

In the 1870s a new design appeared, the double scent-bottle. This was a slim cylindrical bottle with a round or polygonal surface. Some were produced in clear glass, some were coloured dark blue, red, green, or yellow, and some were decorated in the Nailsea style. At each end were silver or plated caps, which were heavily chased or moulded. Some bottles hinged in the middle, and when you opened them there was the grating of a vinaigrette on one side and on the other a recess with a glass-covered photograph. The outer ends had normal hinge- or screw-caps so that either part of the bottle could be filled with scent.

The production of scent bottles continued into the twentieth century, though it became more customary to buy scent in ready-filled bottles from cosmetic houses. These 'package' bottles in themselves have become the object of much decorative skill, and no doubt in the not too distant future they will be sought after by collectors. Some manufacturers supplied scent bottles with rubber bulbs, which could be attached to the top of the bottle to produce a fine spray of scent.

Although some types of scent bottle can be expensive, there are still many cheaper examples, and this is a field in which you could start collecting now without having to mortgage your property for the money!

Victorian wineglasses and vases in opaline and clear glass. At the back an apothecaries' jar with its original contents

Bottles

Who would think that there was any point in collecting old bottles? Well, a great many people around the world evidently do, including a young schoolboy in the north of England, who has thousands – and they are all different. In the United States bottle collecting has become a positive craze, but this is not entirely surprising, for it was there that the mass production of bottles and the marketing of carbonated drinks on a wide scale really began.

Up to about a hundred years ago, drinks like beer, lager, and cider were usually sold in screw- or cork-top stone jars. With the brewer's name in black lettering round the body, they looked very attractive. Then, bottles of glass began to be produced on a commercial scale, though at first they were made by hand. By the end of the nineteenth century the process had been mechanized, and the industry had grown to such an extent that in 1899 28,000 people in the United States were employed in making about 8,000,000 bottles.

Among these were bottles for aerated drinks, like fizzy lemonade, orangeade, and Coca-Cola. The earlier bottlers had a problem keeping the fizz and the freshness in. One of the first solutions was Hiram Codd's bottle, which was sealed by means

Group of decorative bottles, including containers for perfume, cologne, and spirits, and at the front three double scent-bottles

Selection of bottles, including *(far left)* a gin bottle, *(centre back)* a beer bottle, and a torpedo-shaped bottle for mineral water. The blue bottles contained poison

of a glass ball held against a rubber ring by gas pressure. Another was the crown cork bottle, which was securely sealed by a cork-lined metal cap clamped on to a shallow boss on the bottle mouth. There were also screw stoppers and lever stoppers. These forms of closure were used on bottles of many kinds, and in America, for example, Codd's bottles are now much sought after by collectors. They were generally light green in colour, and in the course of manufacture the name of the maker and the contents was embossed on the surface.

People who collect bottles overlook nothing. Torpedo-shaped lemonade bottles of the 1900s, early Guinness bottles, Toledo Lager bottles, gin bottles, and whisky bottles, many of which came in splendid shapes, are all sought after.

Domestic electroplate items in everyday use at the turn of the century

METALWORK

Almost since man has been civilized, he has made tools and ornaments of metal. To begin with they were in copper or bronze (a mixture of copper and tin). Then, in the second millennium BC, the Hittites in Asia Minor discovered how to smelt iron, which is much harder, and so, for tools at all events, more effective. Early man also discovered gold and silver, though in some civilizations, such as those of ancient Mexico and Peru, he did not set the value on them that we do now.

Over the centuries the range of articles made in metal and the variety of base metals and alloys used increased, particularly during the Industrial Revolution.

If we take only the metal goods produced between about 1860 and about 1930, there is a great choice for collecting, and many of these articles are still quite cheap.

Silver and plate

Silver is generally not cheap in any form, but the kind of article which you could get for a pound or two includes cigarette cases, napkin rings, bon-bon dishes, caddy spoons, thimbles, silver-edged brushes and combs, miniature picture frames, hunter watches (see page 32), and sugar tongs. If you are going to make a collection of silver, get a copy of the little pocket book *British and Irish Silver Assay Marks, 1544–1968* by F. Bradbury. This is a first essential, for you will need to check the hallmarks on your purchases. They will establish whether the article is silver and tell you the year of make and the area in Britain (as there were several assay offices) where it was made.

Why not start the easy way? Collect salt spoons. They are all more or less the same size, but I suppose each one is different from the next. Quite apart from the monogram or the crest on the handle, which will be different in every case, the shapes are also variable. When you get tired of salt spoons, cigar and cigarette cases are another line, and they can sometimes be found for small sums. Quite often cigarette cases have become

Silver and plate cutlery, including pickle forks, butter knives, and spoons for marmalade and salt

Some late Victorian silver and plate. The hairbrush and hand mirror are Art Nouveau design in silver, the picture frame is also silver, and the sugar tongs are plated

scratched and dented through constant use, and so can be bought quite cheaply.

In about 1743 silver plate was invented in Sheffield. It was made by fusing a layer of silver on to a thicker layer of copper. After being rolled out, it could be used to make all manner of articles, that at first sight looked like real silver. As it was also a cheaper material, it was not long before many households that hitherto had had to be content with polished copper or brass utensils began to acquire plate dishes, containers, and sets of cutlery. Silver plate was particularly suitable for articles with a large surface area, like trays, tureens, and large rose bowls. It was also marked by the maker's initials and other identification signs, which are in the Bradbury book. Sheffield plate was extremely widely used for nearly a hundred years, until in 1840 the Elkingtons of Birmingham invented the process of coating base metal, usually copper or nickel, with a very thin coat of silver by electrolysis. This was called electroplating, and it dealt a crushing blow to the Sheffield-plate industry, for it was substantially cheaper. Soon a host of articles began to appear in electroplate, usually marked EPNS (electro-plated nickel silver), and some were very well made. Many silver salvers were most beautifully decorated. Of course, the silver wears off, but articles can be resilvered.

Brass and copper

Brass, an alloy of copper and zinc, first appeared in quantity in Britain during the sixteenth century. From the very beginning, a wide selection of domestic articles, from candlesticks and pans to fire irons, was made. The earlier articles showed, by the flaws in their surface, signs of impure mixing and making, and it was not until the eighteenth century that shiny good-quality brass was in widespread use. In Victorian times brass was used for ewers, watering-cans, bells for dray horses (called

It could take some time to amass a collection of thimbles such as this

Some late 19th-century horse brasses and martingales

rumblers), horse brasses, Benares ware (Birmingham-made brass articles with a distinctly oriental flavour), inkpots, doorknockers, fenders, trivets, preserving pans, lamps, hand warmers, and bedsteads. Some brass is inordinately expensive, especially in 'old-world' antique shops in picturesque towns, but in more run-of-the-mill shops it can be found more cheaply. If they are polished up vigorously, brass ornaments are decorative and blend well with beams and rafters.

Copper is a mysterious metal. You can see yourself almost as well in a highly polished copper lid as in a mirror and yet, if you leave the copper for a while, it goes black and then green as it oxidizes, until it reflects nothing at all. It is soft and wears away with cleaning. That is why there is so little copper left more than about 200 years old, except in museums. The Victorians, in fact, are known to have reproduced earlier styles in some quantity. You can see one of the few remaining collections of genuine eighteenth-century copper ware at the Royal Pavilion, Brighton.

Copper was used for coalscuttles, ale measures, warming pans, kettles, and coffeepots. These are now fetching high prices, but from time to time you can get an odd candle holder for about a pound.

Iron

Ironwork is a richer field for collecting in an inexpensive way. Demolition gangs breaking up our grandfathers' houses are still overlooking many collectible things and crushing them among the rubble. Among fixtures and fittings which can make decorative additions to the home, either in their original state or modified for different use, are small fire grates, fire baskets, trivets, fenders, fireguards, fire irons, door porters, flower stands, gridirons, clock jacks, weights, and measures.

Door porters are doorstops. They were made of glass, brass,

Metal articles of the late 19th century. The iron-trivet is steel and the flatiron is painted cast iron. The remaining articles are brass

and cast iron. Those in cast iron are the cheapest and easiest to find. They were in the form of animals, bells, and tall ships, or representations of well-known personalities, real and fictional. A popular model was the one of Jumbo, a famous London Zoo elephant. His name was depicted in raised letters on the stand supporting the model.

You would not, I feel, be very popular with your family if you began to fill the house with iron umbrella-stands, but some of the late Victorian examples are ingenious. I saw one shaped like a dog sitting on a tree stump. The base was in the form of a pile of leaves. In the dog's mouth was a whip with a long cord tied in two bows, one on each side of the animal's head. You put your stick or umbrella through the hoop and rested the ferrule among the leaves.

It is a long time since bronze was used for tools, but it has always been appealing for ornaments. The Victorians liked bronze figures and groups, such as horses and riders, or classical statues. Many of these figures were made in France, Germany, and Italy, where, presumbably, you can still buy them quite cheaply in country districts. As bronze was not cheap, a substitute material, called spelter, was devised, which looked much the same. If you are looking for genuine bronze, you need to get advice on recognizing the difference.

Pewter and Britannia metal

I suppose that everyone has a pewter article somewhere in the house. It may be a tankard with a glass bottom, or perhaps a set of pewter plates. This interesting alloy of tin, lead, copper, and antimony or bismuth looks particularly attractive in country cottages. Early pewter is hard to find and expensive, but after 1824, when it became obligatory to stamp cups and tankards with the capacity of the vessel and the monogram of the monarch, it is said that the quality declined. This later pewter was turned out in bulk and is very collectible. The country-born articles were often well made by rural craftsmen.

If you are collecting pewter, watch out for a very similar but shinier material which is often mistaken for it. This is Britannia metal, itself a pleasant alloy made of tin, copper, and antimony, and mass-produced by a spinning process. It emerged in the middle of the eighteenth century but came into general use a

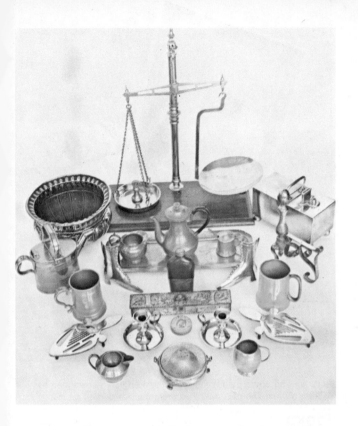

Selection of 19th- and early 20th-century household articles in a variety of metals, including pewter, Britannia metal, brass, copper, iron, and 'tinned metal'

century later, after the name Britannia metal had been patented by Richard Sturges. Earlier pieces had been marked by an X surmounted by a crown. If you see a piece marked E P B M, it means electroplated Britannia metal. This came into use in about 1840, at the time electroplating was introduced, and manufacturers often used Britannia metal as the base for their articles. When the coating wore off, there was still a silvery hue underneath.

Victorian and Edwardian wallpapers, including some designed by William Morris. The gala opera programmes are printed on silk

BOOKS

Many people like to have shelves filled with books. If they can have a row or two of nice old leather-bound volumes with gold lettering, they feel their display is complete. It does not seem to matter to some whether the books are ever read, and in many cases the pages are left uncut.

Although the quality, the binding, and the type of illustrations have varied, books have looked more or less the same for three centuries. They have always been collected and, apart from rare editions, they have usually been relatively inexpensive. Today there are vast quantities of nineteenth-century books, both single volumes and whole sets, which can be found at country sales or in second-hand bookshops for very little money. The complete works of the more prolific novelists of the century, such as Dickens, Trollope, and Balzac, were published in handsomely bound sets, and you can sometimes buy these at almost give-away prices. Cheap single-volume compendia began to appear at the beginning of the present century, but sets continued to be produced for the more fastidious and affluent members of the public.

If you are going to collect books, why not go in for a mixture; a few travel books, some nineteenth-century biographies and memoirs, and a mail order catalogue or two would make an interesting collection. A field not widely exploited at the moment is school textbooks. Think of some of the old faithfuls you had, like Kennedy's *Latin Primer* or Hall and Knight's *Algebra for Beginners*. These were first published in the second half of the nineteenth century!

And have you ever thought of collecting paperbacks? They are not a modern invention. In the first years of the century one could get Tauchnitz editions of most classics and the best modern novels. These were poor-quality paperbacks, which cost no more than a shilling or so.

Collection of 19th-century printed matter. The bound volumes are a set of Dickens' works

Album of early 20th-century cigarette cards from Germany. The print on the right of an Italian uniform is one of a set

CARDS

If you are ever bequeathed trunks full of old albums, or a house whose attic is crammed with seemingly useless items of paper, be very careful before you consign everything to the incinerator. You could be burning pound notes, as it were, for, although there may not be a fortune among the various scraps, there may well be items people want and are willing to buy.

Valentine cards

Like most people today, the Victorians and Edwardians sent Valentine cards. On the whole, their cards were more elaborately designed, though the poems and messages were hardly less trite than those of today. They were printed chiefly by lithography, then a new technique, and of the many Valentines produced, some were most intricate. There were cards with simulated lace edges or prettily coloured pictures, and some were even decorated with dried flowers. One rare card is the type which by pulling a cord on the front is converted into a cage. Valentine cards are not easy to collect because they are fragile. There are specialists, however, off Charing Cross Road and in an arcade off the south side of Piccadilly.

Postcards

The Victorians were enthusiastic postcard writers. When photography became a household experience, stationery manufacturers produced photograph postcards, at first in black and white, and later in colour, of almost anything they could dream up: famous resorts, buildings, and landscapes; celebrated soldiers, statesmen, members of the royal family, actors, and explorers. Some of these were unusual in that they were raised, that is, the prominent features of, say, Lord Kitchener stood out from the background. This almost three-dimensional aspect was an interesting development.

Picture postcards began not in Britain but on the Continent, particularly in Austria. People soon began to collect them. A favourite pastime was to build up a volume of autographed

Various cards and posters; railway posters are in great demand today, and some firms are reproducing them

cards of famous stage personalities. Henry Irving and Ellen Terry probably signed more than anybody else, and neither of these signatures is worth very much today.

At the beginning of this century the first risqué joke cards appeared, and, not unnaturally, these have been very popular ever since. Early 'dirty' postcards are getting hard to find.

Cigarette cards

Another kind of card which was first made about a century ago is the cigarette card. In October, 1972, there was a sale of cigarette cards in many lots, some of which fetched extremely high prices. Popular subjects of the earliest sets were kings and queens, and generals, while later series included aeroplanes, cars, national flags, uniforms, and flowers. Each card carried some information about the illustration on the other side.

If you do come across some cards, try collecting a few more. There are now cigarette-card collecting organizations and even a journal called *Cigarette Card News*.

Stereoscope cards

In the 1950s did you ever go to those 3-D films which you had to view through a pair of red-and-yellow glasses handed to you at the door? It was the latest thing in films, until someone developed Cinemascope and thereby produced much the same result without the glasses. Well, in late Victorian times you may not have been able to see any films, but you could have your own 3-D show at home. For a few shillings you could buy a stereoscope. This was a strip of wood, with an eyepiece at one end and at the other end a slot, into which you inserted cards. The cards consisted of a pair of identical photographs set at a very slight angle to each other. By adjusting the distance between the eyepiece and the card you got a three-dimensional view of the picture. Stereoscopes are not easy to find, but the cards, which offer great variety of subject matter, often turn up at sales and in junk shops. If you were to collect the cards, you could soon make your own stereoscope.

Surrounding the viewer are some Victorian stereoscope cards, both black and white and colour, and below these a selection of Valentine cards

NEWSPAPERS AND MAGAZINES

'Last Friday a brute called Jones sold his wife at an auction in Dorchester for five pounds . . .'

So runs the beginning of a short newspaper article in a splendid tome of cuttings left to me by my grandmother some years ago. Filled from cover to cover with an astonishing range of cuttings taken mainly from West Country newspapers of the early nineteenth century, this book has been an endless source of fun and interest to my family. What happened, we have often wondered, to the unfortunate five-pound wife? Was this terse clipping, only six lines in all, the source of Thomas Hardy's tragic story, *The Mayor of Casterbridge*?

Newspapers are most valuable social documents, and collecting whole newspapers or cuttings from earlier days is a fascinating recreation. They are not often found in shops or sales, except as collections, like the book I have mentioned, or unless they are well-known editions of papers reporting an event of national importance. At the British Empire Exhibition in 1924, for instance, you could buy reproduction copies of *The Times* of November 1805, which reported the death of Nelson at Trafalgar, but an original *Times* of that date would be extremely hard to find.

You can look for other papers or cuttings, and, if you want to specialize, the field is wide open.

Magazines were an innovation of the nineteenth century, and by the end of the century there was already a wide range available to readers. There was *The Strand Magazine*, which serialized the first Sherlock Holmes stories. There was *Boys Own Paper*. There was *Illustrated London News*, now well over a hundred years old, whose early pictures were fine lifelike engravings. An issue of 1855, for example, shows the portable hospital buildings put up in Renkioi, Turkey, for British troops in the Crimean War. These buildings – sensational in their day – were the brainchild of Isambard Brunel, and were but one more manifestation of his astonishing genius.

And of course there were volumes – and volumes – of *Punch*. Consigned even fifteen years ago to paper pulpers, they are now prized. If you see a collection covering, say, five or six years' issues, buy it.

(top to bottom) Book of newspaper cuttings, bound set of *The Strand Magazine* open at the first Sherlock Holmes story ever published, early 20th-century *Boy's Own Annual*, copy of the *Boy's Own Paper*

Oleograph of a hunting scene, c. 1890, and *(below)* 'cowscape' (picture of cows in a pastoral setting) by W. S. Cooper

PICTURES

When paintings like Titian's *Death of Actaeon* fetch over £1,000,000 at a saleroom, how, you may wonder, can one begin to collect pictures? You may also wonder whether that old oil painting you have of a washerwoman bending over a tub in a scullery is not some masterpiece of the seventeenth-century Dutch school of painting and so worth a fortune. You are right if you feel that the world of pictures is a tricky one, full of hopes and disappointments, expertise and ignorance, genuine work and forgery.

It is probably wisest to get it clear at the start that the likelihood of picking up an undiscovered masterpiece is now almost non-existent. So, unless you have a lot of money, you will have to limit yourself to pictures of the nineteenth century: water-colours, prints, and reproductions of old masters. Make no mistake, though, there are plenty of very pleasing pictures to be bought for little money. For the most part, they will probably have little artistic merit in the opinion of the experts, and they may not be an investment in the short term.

By the nineteenth century there were many colleges and schools of art, through which hundreds of students passed, many of them becoming quite competent and successful artists. Ten years ago, I bought a large portfolio of miscellaneous drawings and watercolours. It was thrown in with a lot of books. The subjects ranged from portrait heads to old castles, fishing to street scenes, classical statues to waterfalls. None of them was framed, but I have put some in inexpensive Victorian frames and they look well enough.

Go into a junk shop and ask to see a portfolio of pictures. You will be shown a host of subjects: huge black and white engravings of classical or theatrical females; copies of water colours of moral stories, such as the famous one of a hurt-looking husband leaning against the mantelpiece as his wife confesses some awful misdemeanour; oleographs of hunting scenes; copies of Lady Elizabeth Butler's famous panoramic canvasses of well-known battles; and reproductions of

19th-century watercolour and copy of a Raphael painting. The woodcut on the right is by Nicholson, one of the Beggarstaff Brothers

(left) Floral felt appliqué picture on velvet, and *(right)* late 19th-century child's sampler

world-famous pictures like *The Last Supper*. Quite often, you can find attractive yellowish maplewood or satinwood frames containing, amongst a wide variety of other subjects, colour pictures of famous race horses.

There was a great vogue for woven silk pictures in the nineteenth century. Scenes might be rustic, classical, or domestic, and were intricately woven in different coloured threads. Sometimes the glass in the frame was painted black round the edges to produce either a square or an oval shape, and the effect was to heighten the colours of the picture. It was Thomas Stevens of Coventry who used the improved Jacquard loom to produce woven silk pictures, called Stevengraphs. These embraced a multitude of subjects, including Leda and the Swan, hunting scenes, railway scenes, and the Oxford and Cambridge Boat Race. Usually, they were roughly the same size – nearly 9 inches by 5 inches – and were stamped with his name. About fifteen years ago Stevengraphs could be bought for shillings, but now they fetch up to £100 or more, according to the subject, and one saleroom in London specializes in auctions of Stevengraphs. If Stevengraphs are beyond your means, less expensive woven silk pictures are available. The technique continued in the present century up to the First World War. During the war the flags and emblems of the various countries involved were illustrated in woven silk on postcards, which were sometimes sold for war charities. You can occasionally find these cards for as little as 25p to 50p.

Samplers are also a field for collectors. These are pieces of linen or canvas on which children used to learn to sew by embroidering their name, age, the alphabet, and some verses of a hymn or poem in different coloured threads. Samplers were first seen in the eighteenth century in Britain and America, and they continued to be produced right up to the 1900s. They can cost under ten pounds.

Embroidered silk picture with a black surround

Victorian jet jewellery

JEWELLERY

At first sight, it may seem incongruous to include jewellery in a book on collecting inexpensive antiques, since any jewellery worth having, one might think, would be beyond the income bracket of most of those to whom this book is directed. But there is, in fact, a wide selection of cheap gems in interesting and attractive settings made in a variety of metals, including bronze, copper, pinchbeck (an alloy that looks like gold), iron, electroplate silver, and rolled gold. The range of jewellery made included everything that is made today, as well as a number of items which are no longer so popular, such as hatpins, lockets, watch holders, chokers, tie pins, and scarf pins. These articles were generally produced in some quantity, so that even the humblest household could afford them.

Let us look at brooches. These have been made almost since the beginnings of civilization. They are nearly always decorative, and periodically they have also been used as badges to signify rank, family, trade, profession, or even supporters' club — supporters for different teams of charioteers in ancient Rome and Constantinople wore brooches. In particularly superstitious days, brooches were worn to fend off evil spirits. In the period we are dealing with, they were almost entirely decorative, though badges of rank, employment, and so forth, were made in great profusion. Cameo brooches made of semi-precious stones, shell, or glass set in gold or gilt surrounds were fashionable for most of the period. Cameos were also employed in other jewellery, such as rings. Coral brooches were worn; these consisted of clusters of coral strands and looked like minute mop heads. Brooches were also made of ivory, mother-of-pearl, and semiprecious stones, like turquoise, jade, and cornelian.

Some Victorian jewellery: *(top left)* Art Nouveau silver ring, *(centre)* coral and mother-of-pearl brooch, *(bottom right)* pair of amber drop earrings

Jewel box overflowing with Victorian brooches, necklaces, and rings of gold, pearls, garnets, turquoise, jet, and agate

The variety of jewellery is so great that only a glance can be attempted in these pages. One or two lines which were fashionable are still in demand today. Much jewellery, for example, was made in jet, a black compact coal. It came into its own as a symbol of grief, when, at the end of 1861, Prince Albert died and the nation was plunged into mourning. Of course, the general public came out of mourning for Albert long before the queen did, and jet then became fashionable as a decorative stone, without this lugubrious association. Necklaces and earrings were perhaps the best liked pieces. Although a great deal of jet jewellery was made, it seems that there is not much of it about now. Possibly people of later generations threw it away.

Another material used for jewellery by the Victorians was amber, often regarded – erroneously – as valuable; it is not as rare as that. A fossilized yellow resin, amber is found mainly in Scandinavia and on the Baltic coast of the U.S.S.R. It has also been found in Britain, and there are some beaches that are well known for it. Its softness makes it easy to carve and shape. In the last years of the nineteenth century, it was used to add the final decorative touches to many articles. You will find, for example, Art Nouveau figures of silver, with amber beads on the extremities. It is quite cheap to buy, as long as you call the bluff of the dealer who tells you that it is rare. If you are not sure, get the advice of a modern jeweller.

Art Nouveau jewellery is now very much sought after. Art Nouveau was a reaction against conventional Victorian design with its constant revivals of historical styles: 'Gothic', 'Renaissance', 'Classical'. Its exponents tried to invent a completely fresh style, hence Art Nouveau – 'new art'. Jewellery provided an obvious medium for experiment, and much that is typical of Art Nouveau design – asymmetry, sinuous lines, flower, bird, and animal motifs – was incorporated into the jewellery produced at the time. Some of the results were rather weird, even frightening, but at the same time strangely beautiful.

Art Nouveau is really a field for collecting in its own right, and there is a chapter about it (see page 138).

The popularity of the Victorian cameo was matched by that of the locket. Here, tiny pictures show three generations of the same family

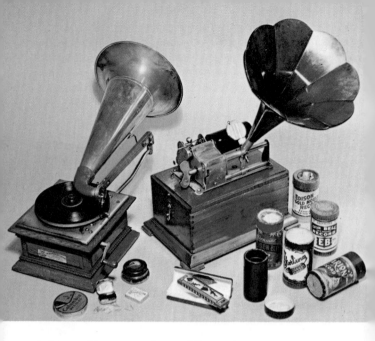

Early turntable gramophone, c. 1900, and *(right)* French Pathé phonograph and cylinders. In front a 1930s mouth organ

MUSICAL ITEMS

Musical instruments are a tempting field for collecting, for there are few junk shops that do not have at least one dented old cornet, battered violin, its strings all broken or missing, or cheap recorder whose mouthpiece is pitted with teeth marks. There are two antique dealers in the village next to mine (population about 400) and both have various musical instruments. Neither expects to make a quick sale, but the instruments add to the variety of articles on show. If you are going to pursue this type of collecting to its logical conclusion, then you may feel you have to embrace the whole gamut of things musical. This can mean including polyphons, gramophones, phonographs, pianolas, musical boxes, barrel organs, and mouth organs. Now these are going to take up a lot of room but, provided you have the space, why not make this your field for collecting, especially if you are musical yourself?

The polyphon was our grandfathers' jukebox or nickelodeon. The mechanism was in a glass-fronted cabinet, which was fixed to the wall, usually in places of public entertainment, like taverns, and was operated by a coin in the slot. For a penny, a steel disc dotted with perforations would rotate, causing small metal lugs to drop down and thus strike a series of metal keys in an order which produced a popular tune, probably a favourite music hall song or an air from a Gilbert and Sullivan opera. These splendid instruments can still be found, but they are no longer cheap, unless of course they are beyond repair.

The earliest home record-player was the phonograph, which was invented by Edison in the 1890s. It consisted of a smallish box surmounted by a spindle. On this you slotted a black cylinder, which was the record. Using a handle on the side of the box, you wound up the motor and lowered a lever containing a needle and a slot on to the edge of the cylinder. Into

Home polyphon

Coin-operated barrel organ of the kind found in bars and cafes at the beginning of the century

the slot you inserted a horn of metal, papier-mâché, or even cardboard. Then you released the catch, and the cylinder turned. The quality of the recording was not at all good by our standards, but at the time it must have seemed something of a miracle. Phonographs can be bought for about twenty pounds, and for that I would expect a small supply of cylinders in cardboard cartons to be included.

Have you ever played a pianola? This is an upright piano, inside which is a mechanism that plays all the notes and operates the pedals for you. All you have to do is to simulate the actions and operate a foot pump to unwind the perforated roll, which activates the mechanism. There were rolls for almost every well-known piece of classical or contemporary music.

There cannot have been many boys in the 1930s who did not have at least one mouth organ. I well remember wanting one first in 1937. I was given a small one at Christmas, but soon wanted the next size up, which was about 9 inches long. Having been given one of these, however, I was still not content and I campaigned for a chromatic model. This type of mouth organ has a button at one side, which when pressed moves a slide across the pipes and alters the notes by a semitone, enabling one to produce all the notes of both major and minor scales. The best-known maker was Honner of Germany. I have not seen a prewar chromatic mouth organ for years but I should think there must be a few about, and you can certainly find the simpler kind in junk shops.

In Victorian and Edwardian times, when musical evenings were still a popular form of home entertainment, sheet music was in great demand. The unbound sheets were usually enclosed in a decorative cover, which often bore a print or sketch illustrating the theme or mood of the song inside. Some top-rate illustrators were engaged to produce these covers, among them Alfred Concanen, whose designs were so numerous as to warrant a collection of their own. Sheet music covers can be found quite cheaply in many bookshops.

Selection of sheet music of popular music-hall songs of the 1900s

Among the early electrical household appliances illustrated here is a Telechron, an American clock with self-starting motor

ELECTRICAL APPARATUS

Supplies of electricity for domestic use began to reach consumers in America and Western Europe during the 1880s. This was accompanied by a spate of inventions of household electrical goods. The two leading inventors were the American, Thomas Edison (1847–1931), and the Scot, Lord Kelvin (1824–1907).

Among the first innovations were various forms of electric lighting. Ceiling lights, which could often be raised or lowered by means of weights and pulleys, were probably earlier than wall fixtures, but to begin with were somewhat cumbersome. The earliest filament lamps are rare, and are generally museum pieces, but early twentieth-century bulbs can be found in old houses due for demolition. They are usually threaded at the socket end, for the bayonet fitting did not come in until 1930.

It was not until the twentieth century that electrical appliances were marketed on really national scales. Electric cookers and ovens appeared, as well as the first electric fires – open filaments mounted in vertical or horizontal wire-framed pedestals, some of which had attachments for keeping kettles warm. The two- three- and four-bar fires that we have today are not so very different from the cast-iron framed models of the 1905 to 1920 period. These older fires can be found cheaply, but, if you intend to use them, you should have them carefully checked by a good electrician.

Vacuum cleaners first appeared in the 1920s. Even if in working order, they are not very effective now, but they would be an unusual investment.

Marconi had first demonstrated the possibilities of wireless in the 1890s, but broadcasting on a national scale did not begin until the 1920s. This came about largely through the work done by many amateur enthusiasts, who built their own receiver sets. These early receivers began as simple crystal sets, consisting principally of a galena crystal, which was flicked with a thin strand of copper wire, called a whisker, and a pair of earphones. The crystal was soon superseded by a detector valve, and the earphones by a loud speaker. These later sets were housed in a cabinet. Although not very attractive, they were, by the 1930s, producing soft gentle tones which cannot always be matched by modern sets.

Pictured here are some of the inventions which revolutionized communications in the 20th century

Cast shop's bell and early cash register

MECHANICAL ITEMS

For anyone with a mechanical turn of mind, there were several articles invented in the latter part of the nineteenth century which would prove both interesting and profitable to collect. Among these I would list early cash registers and typewriters.

The first cash register was made by Ritty of Ohio in 1879. It was a simple machine, which merely registered the amount of the sale. A little later emerged the till which punched a hole in a roll of paper, that was divided into columns. This machine was produced by the National Cash Register Company, which for some time monopolized the manufacture of cash tills. Tills of the early 1900s in brass or highly polished metal, with a loud bell and white enamel keys, are fetching good prices today. If you want to get one a little more cheaply, find out whether an old-established departmental store in a provincial town has recently been taken over. If so, it may be due for modernization, and there may be one or two of these old tills ready to be disposed of. While looking for a till, see if you can find one of those splendid cable-operated change apparati with the cylinders which winged their way across the ceiling with your change and a receipt.

Typewriters were dreamed about in the eighteenth century, but the first successful machine was made by Sholes of Milwaukee in 1873. It cost $125 and was marketed by the Remington Company, which is still a famous name in typewriters. This first machine and its immediate successors were rather complex, and in fact you could not see what you had typed until you had finished. These early models are rare and they fetch high prices. By the end of the century, Underwoods, another famous name, were producing the first of the typewriters which heralded the machines we know today. They had four banks of keys, a roller, and various shift levers, and you could see what you were writing. One early portable typewriter was built so that it hinged in the middle. You folded one end (the keyboard) on to the other, and then tucked the machine away into a small case.

Oliver typewriter made at the turn of the century and upright telephone made after the First World War

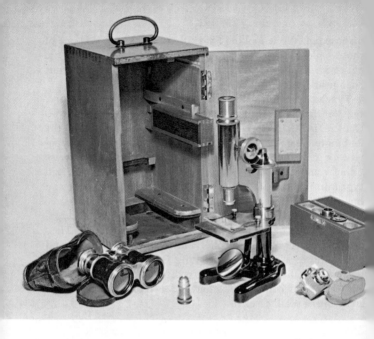

(left) Pair of French opera glasses, and Edwardian brass microscope with box and accessories

PHOTOGRAPHIC AND OPTICAL EQUIPMENT

Photography is not a cheap pastime. Collecting old photographic equipment, however, can be surprisingly cheap.

Cameras were first produced on a commercial scale towards the end of the nineteenth century. They usually came in wooden cases, which were lined with baize or velvet and fitted with special slots for lenses, lens covers, and other gadgets. I have seen these in antique shops, generally dating from about 1900 onwards, and they seem to cost twenty pounds or so.

Not long before the First World War, the Eastman Kodak Company of Rochester, New York, produced a very small folding camera. When closed, it was about 1 inch thick, $4\frac{1}{2}$ inches high, and $2\frac{1}{2}$ inches wide. It had several refinements: you could adjust the shutter to two different speeds: 1/25 and 1/50 sec, increase the aperture for poor light conditions, and you could also vary the focal length to range from *Close-up Portrait* to *Clouds/Marine*. In 1914 this delightful little camera could be bought in Britain for only five shillings, but I think it could cost five pounds today.

When photography came within the reach of the man in the street, everybody wanted pictures of themselves, their families, and their homes, to say nothing of that holiday by the sea. You can find photographs of the 1880s to 1920s at sales and in shops. They are marvellous documents of how our grandfathers lived and enjoyed themselves. Photograph albums also come up for sale, and they can tell quite a story.

Cameras were very popular with the Victorians, who had a passion for keeping a record of events. They already knew about instruments like telescopes and microscopes, and these still appear in antique shops all over the country. Most naval officers had telescopes, and most medical students had microscopes. The lenses and working parts were most beautifully made, and in many cases they are still perfectly serviceable.

Late Victorian studio camera

BAROMETERS AND WEATHER VANES

Many people go a long way to find old instruments connected with the weather, and among those which are sought after are barometers. The barometer was invented in 1642 by Torricelli, who had been Galileo's secretary, and it consisted of vertical glass tubes containing mercury, the level of which rose and fell according to the prevailing atmospheric pressure, thereby giving one a rough guide to the weather prospects. These tubes came to be enclosed in thin rectangular boxes and were known as stick barometers.

A later development was the banjo barometer, which was introduced towards the end of the eighteenth century. This is the type you see most frequently in shops and houses. The rise and fall of the mercury is registered on a dial by a large hand, which swings from left to right. Mounted above the barometer was an alcohol or mercury room-thermometer.

The top of the barometer was often a classical pediment, and the front of the case had inlays of various kinds, most notably shell motifs. These pieces were Georgian, and today they can be found for about thirty pounds or so. The basic style continued well into the last decades of the nineteenth century, although the graceful Georgian lines gave way to more contemporary Victorian ideas.

It appears that people in America are collecting old weather vanes. These are very interesting because so many of the designs record the kind of problems that faced the local communities where they were made. You will not be surprised to hear that one recurrent theme was that of a Red Indian portrayed in various postures, such as with an arrow through his heart, or mounted on a horse standing on an arrow. Weather vanes are in demand in Britain as well, though British designs are perhaps not as exciting. The way to collect weather vanes is to visit old-established forges which have been in the same family for some generations and see what the present blacksmith can offer you. Of course, many reproductions are being manufactured, but these are made of mild steel rather than wrought iron.

Some barometers; on the right a Georgian one of the banjo type

GAMES AND TOYS

Each generation produces a mass of new ideas and invention
for games and toys, many of which quickly date and disappear
This leaves the field wide open for the collector; he can eve
include articles made during and immediately after th
Second World War and still find that they have become rare
In 1938 I was given a set of lead models of French ships: grea
battleships, like the *Dunkerque* and the *Richelieu*, or th
Surcouf, then the largest submarine in the world. Where woul
one find these today? I have never met anyone who eve
remembers this particular set. But among the games and toy
that date and vanish, a handful remains, reissued every genera
tion in some new and glamorized form.

Take games. Chess, board games, and card games have been
played for centuries. Chess sets took many forms, the piece
sometimes bearing little resemblance to those we use today
although the rules and techniques were the same. All kind
of materials were used, including wood, ivory, porcelain
metal, and stone. Of course, the wood and the ivory sets o

Solitaire board, ludo set, lead chess pieces, cribbage board and
playing cards

In front of the Victorian toy theatre are a set of American alphabet building blocks and a wooden jigsaw puzzle

the last century are the cheapest, and they can be bought for ten pounds or so. Many are of the Staunton design, so named after a British chess champion of the early nineteenth century.

Other board games of the last hundred years which are still produced today are snakes and ladders, ludo, draughts, and solitaire. You can often get a good solitaire board and marbles at country sales or jumble sales. Ludo boards a century old may be scarce because the cardboard was not durable. But people are collecting board games of the 1930s, for these are more plentiful. One game introduced at that time was Monopoly, which has become one of the best known and most widely played games in the world. Over the years, snakes and ladders boards acquired some wonderful designs and colours. It was almost worth falling down the snake from number 91 to number 39 to trace the gorgeous sinewy colours of the great boa constrictor which weaved its way across the board.

Another perennial favourite is the jigsaw puzzle. Early puzzles were made of wood and were usually packed in attractive wooden boxes. The royal family, war scenes, the countryside, ships of sail and stream – these were some of the more popular subjects for the pictures on jigsaw puzzles.

Before the war – and soon afterwards – many firms had their name printed on the back of playing card packs which were given away. These packs were almost all the same size and quality, and only the design and the name on the back differed. A collection of these would be both interesting and unusual, and you could also include patience cards, which were smaller.

The great variety of games is almost equalled by the range of toys given to our grandfathers at Christmas, on birthdays, and when they had been particularly good! The best toys of the late nineteenth century were made in Germany and Switzerland. Models of people, animals, buildings, and vehicles were produced in wood or tin, and tin soldiers were very much in demand. In the years between the world wars tin

Box of lead soldiers of c. 1890, and *(below)* French tin soldier of 1910

Early Victorian dolls' house with its original wallpapers, furniture, and fittings

and lead military models were produced in abundance. You could collect soldiers of different regiments or nationalities, or build up war sets of working searchlights, howitzers that fired caps and discharged shells or matchsticks, and tanks with caterpillar tracks. Model cars were also tremendous fun. Just before the Second World War, the Germans made two interesting remote control cars: the Schuco and the Spiro. The Schuco was a clockwork saloon car. It was controlled by a steering wheel connected by a thin wire to a rubber hose, which fitted on a spike in the top of the car. The control on the Spiro was a rubber bulb, which pumped air down a tube into a slot in the roof of the car. Each squeeze moved the car, but it could be quite exhausting getting a car to traverse the length of a room!

Children also love model buildings, especially toy theatres and dolls' houses, and Victorian dolls' houses have rightly excited the admiration of people all over the world.

Various articles of treen, including a nest of boxes

TREEN

Treen is an old word meaning wooden. It is now used as a collective term for small articles made of wood. The variety embraced by the word is enormous and includes pepper-mills, cigarette boxes, flower troughs, napkin rings, punchbowls lined with metal, platters, porringers, ladles, salad servers, bowls, puzzle moneyboxes, eggcups, spice boxes, lemon squeezers, pails, glove stretchers, potato mashers, spoons, mouse-traps, colanders, back scratchers, and nutcrackers.

The more decorative articles for the drawing room or bedroom were polished, lacquered, painted, or inlaid with coloured woods, ivory, mother-of-pearl, or coloured glass. The earlier kitchen tools were shined up rather than polished and today will be rough, stained, chipped, and scorched, revealing a lot of use in days gone by.

If you want your collection to be especially varied, look out for unusual objects, such as truncheons, miniature furniture, items in chip carving, spinning wheels (but beware of modern imitations), or small hanging bookshelves.

Truncheons were emblazoned with the force's arms and the name of the district, and were ebonized or lacquered. Miniature furniture was usually made by apprentices, who were instructed by the master craftsmen to make a certain piece in miniature before trying to make the real article. Good apprentice-pieces are rare and expensive, but there are still many simpler articles to be found for a few pounds.

Chip carving is lightly chipped ornamentation on wood surfaces. It was originally done on late medieval furniture, but the skill, which is not a very intricate one, was taken up again towards the end of the last century for decorating small articles.

Small hanging shelves can still be found in junk shops and country sales. They are sometimes decorated with crude carving on the shelf fronts, or adorned with fretwork or pierced corner-pieces where the shelves meet the sides. They are particularly suitable for small books and china ornaments. I do think smaller Staffordshire figures look better on these slightly ornamental shelves than on plain white wood.

Treen boot trees, glove stretchers, and decorated trinket boxes

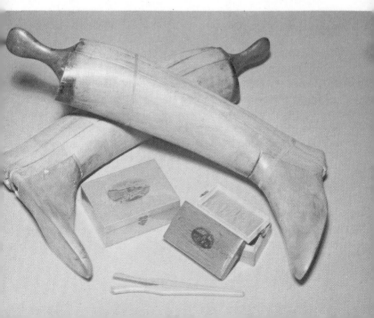

(above and right) These two articles of Tunbridge ware illustrate well the technique of this wood mosaic

TUNBRIDGE WARE

This is the name given to an exclusively English form of wood mosaic, which was first made by local craftsmen in and around Tunbridge Wells in Kent. Tunbridge Wells had become a fashionable place to take the waters early in the seventeenth century, and, as most people indulging in this healthy pastime were in effect on holiday in the town, with money to burn, local craftsmen soon began to take advantage and manufacture items made by this process, which is noted for the great variety of woods and colours used.

Briefly, thin strips of wood of different colours and grain were glued together and pressed down tightly in blocks. When the glue was dry, the blocks were cut across the strips (like carving a joint or slicing a loaf) to produce thin sheets of pat-terned wood, which were then applied as veneer to a great variety of objects, such as workboxes, candlesticks, writing boxes, jewel boxes, barometers, trays, and tea caddies.

As the decades went by, the craftsmen improved their techniques and used a wider range of woods and colourings, so that by the nineteenth century Tunbridge ware had become one of the best-known forms of wood decoration. In Victorian times the scale on which pieces were made increased, and the result is that, while the skill remained an intricate one, a multitude of articles was turned out. This means that there is still a great deal of Tunbridge ware about and it can be bought quite cheaply.

One of the last firms making Tunbridge ware was Boyce, Brown and Kemp, whose craftsmen were still producing articles after the First World War. It is hard to tell the age of items, partly because of the heavy use to which they have been put. A collection of known twentieth-century creations by Boyce, Brown and Kemp would be worth accumulating, but it would be necessary to be sure of the source of the articles. You could do worse than begin in Tunbridge Wells or its neighbour, Tonbridge.

Collection of Victorian and Edwardian kitchen utensils, including earthenware jars, mincers, a griddle, and a grater

HOUSEHOLD ARTICLES

The Victorian and Edwardian upper and upper middle classes were, on the whole, wealthy and had a lot of time to spend their riches. They made a great occasion of eating and drinking – an Edwardian dinner party, for example, quite often lasted from about eight o'clock until after midnight, during which time eight or nine courses would be consumed. Consequently, their kitchens were well equipped with all manner of gadgets which were geared to producing the great variety of dishes they ate, a variety stimulated by the appearance of Mrs Beeton's *Book of Household Management*, which contained 4000 recipes and was a perennial success. Many of the gadgets were also labour saving, for the preparation of an eight-course meal was quite an undertaking.

These kitchen gadgets and utensils were often mass produced. Until a few years ago, such articles were considered rubbish, but, miraculously, they did not all vanish on scrap heaps, and whole shops are now given over to their sale.

Perhaps the first articles you think of in association with the kitchen are saucepans. These were produced in quantity in brass and copper lined inside with tin. Some had lids, usually flat, with a small hand grip in the centre, which was a constant cause of singed fingers, as very few insulated grips were produced before the twentieth century. Saucepans of this kind can be found in many shops.

The sort of items you now have in aluminium or plastic, such as jelly moulds, mixing bowls, cheese graters, and egg lifters, the Victorians had in copper, iron, china, or wood. The illustration shows some ceramic jelly moulds.

Among the gadgets were coffee grinders, which were made in many shapes, all achieving the same object. Most common, probably, was the type which was affixed to the wall and consisted of a china or wooden container for the beans, with a glass receptacle slotted below the holder. The handle projected forwards or sideways. The china containers were often gaily decorated. I have one in nineteenth-century English delftware,

Victorian spice box, complete with nutmeg grater, and ceramic jelly moulds of various sizes

with a blue windmill and boat motif. These grinders gave some meaning to the term 'freshly ground'. There is a very famous coffee shop and snack-bar in Old Brompton Road, London, which has a splendid collection of these and many other household articles and outdoor implements displayed on its shelves and walls.

Some people may feel they are being original if they have a kitchen shelf crammed full of tins and jars of spices for exotic dishes. In fact, spices have been part of European cooking for centuries. In the Middle Ages they were kept in wooden boxes or drawers; in the nineteenth century in tins or jars. Spice tins, such as the one illustrated here, were often divided into compartments for the different spices, and contained a grater for things like nutmeg. These can be found today and are worth collecting because of the great variety of shapes and sizes, and, of course, they can still be used. They are often painted black on the outside, and many still retain the aroma of the spices they once contained.

Among the many other kitchen appurtenances which are collectible – but you would need a lot of space for them – are old coal stoves, cast-iron gas cookers, early iceboxes, particularly the American type, and early English refrigerators. Some of the Electrolux refrigerators manufactured in the 1920s and 1930s are still in good working order. We have one, which my family swears has in its time been run on electricity (main), gas, calor gas, electricity (home generated) – everything except nuclear power – and it is still absolutely reliable. It is over forty years old. A neighbour has an identical one, of like age and in like condition, and my father has a larger version of the same model, also working well. None of us would get more than a few pence for the scrap, yet if I were offered another one I would buy it.

Smaller articles which can be bought for next to nothing, or even found on scrap heaps or demolition sites are flatirons, iron stands, old kettles and trivets, and iron vegetable-racks. Items even as late as the 1930s have collecting value today.

Kitchen gadgetry was no less diverse in Victorian times than it is today. Among the items illustrated here are a pestle and mortar, a cheese mould, butter printers, a food warmer, and a steak mallet

Edwardian knife-grinder

After all, a large proportion of the population does not remember ever seeing a flatiron – except in a period film!

Some Victorian and Edwardian table knives were made of iron or steel, which turned black after use. To solve this problem, knife grinders and sharpeners were invented. They were cased in wood or iron plate and had a winding handle. The blades were inserted through slots and sandwiched between pads impregnated with fine carborundum. By turning the handle, the stains were removed. In 1963 I picked up a small iron-plate one in the Portobello Road for £1, and the other day I saw a larger wooden-cased one for only £3.

Another item you may consider collecting is huge cups and saucers. They were first made in the mid-nineteenth century, mainly, though not entirely, as jokes or for souvenirs, and many ceramic makers produced them, notably, Wedgwood, Spode, Coalport, and even Derby. I began to collect these in 1970, really as a sort of investment, in the hope that one day a mad American might come and buy the lot. And so it happened, as I mention later (see page 101).

Among the more attractive designs was the cup shaped like a chamber-pot and bearing a picture of a river and windmill scene superscribed by the refrain *Take ye a cup o' kindness for Auld Lang Syne*. I had four of these, all differing in colour and in the finer details of the picture. Another was a huge $3\frac{1}{2}$-pint capacity cup, which on one side had the gold inscription *A present from Southend* underneath two delightfully coloured flying pheasants, and on the other, also under some birds, the remark *I am not greedy but I like a lot*.

These big cups and saucers can still be bought for two to three pounds. I did not pay more, and you should try to knock down the price if more is asked. They were mass produced and are not fine, thin, or beautiful. Some china manufacturers are reproducing them today, and I have seen one or two with prints of the famous *Cries of London* series.

Victorian sewing machine with enamel and mother-of-pearl inlay, together with a lady's companion containing tools for every need

SANITARY WARE

Perhaps you would not think there was any great enthusiasm for Victorian and Edwardian bathroom and w.c. ware, but, quite apart from chamber-pots, there is now a great demand for all kinds of toilet fittings and appurtenances.

The heavily decorated lavatory pedestals which, fifteen years or more ago, were ripped out with no compunction when huge Victorian houses were being pulled down to make way for blocks of flats or motorways are now the treasured relics of a leisurely bygone age. Dolphins, dragons, fishes, birds – these are some of the motifs which decorate pedestals made by such famous ceramic makers as Doulton, Minton, and Worcester. But, as a rule, pedestals of this kind are no longer cheap, though you might just get one on a demolition site in a small town by offering the gang foreman a five pound note.

If you want to make a collection of toilet ware, look out for simpler things, such as soap dishes, or ewers and basins. They were produced in an immense range of patterns and colours and can be collected in sets or as individual items.

'The Sanitas wash-down closet'

Early 20th-century toilet set with matching jug, bowl, soap dish, shaving mug, and chamber-pot

Unless badly damaged, sets made by the principal ceramic manufacturers are now fetching ten pounds or more in country sales. Some sets include slop pails with perforated lids and basketware handles, and these make very attractive flowerpots.

Also a part of toilet sets were pairs of chamber-pots, which are now very popular and collected in their own right, whether in pairs or singly. Earlier in this book I mentioned the American who bought my collection of large cups and saucers. It really started with my collecting chamber-pots. Every Saturday I visited the same market stall in Saffron Walden and bought one or two decorated chamber-pots, usually for about ten to fifteen shillings. Within a year I had fifty, including one with a lid and one with two handles. One day an American dealer called, and I showed him the range of chamber-pots and big cups and saucers. He said he would take the lot – and at an agreeable price. You can still get chamber-pots for fifty pence and could quite easily do the same as I did.

Garden bench with cast iron sides, and wooden slat seat and back

GARDEN FURNITURE

So many antiques today are found inside the home that it is easy to overlook the furniture and ornaments specially made for the garden. This is odd when one remembers that the British are the most enthusiastic gardeners in the world. In Victorian and Edwardian times, much attention was given to enhancing and decorating gardens with statues, stone seats, wrought- or cast-iron benches, tea-tables on iron tripods, and ornaments of many kinds. These ornaments, which included Grecian urns, pedestals, rectangular decorated flower-boxes, horses, lions, unicorns, caryatids, little boys with dolphins, and cherubs holding scallop shells, were made of stone, plaster, concrete, and terracotta, or, if you could afford it, marble. Many of the statues of Roman and Greek design were in the cheaper Parian marble, and a great variety of materials was used for bird-tables and birdbaths.

Fountains were very popular, and many ornaments were bored out and fitted with pipes for connecting to the water mains. Water gushed into scallop-shell troughs from lions' mouths fixed to the wall.

Some of these ornaments can be unnecessarily expensive, especially if you go to those dealers who specialize. They believe they are on to a limited supply for a big market and so put up the prices. Profits run to several hundred per cent (according to one unashamed dealer I know). The answer is to look in country junk shops and see what you can find. I bought a rather nice slatted wood bench with scroll back and sides for two pounds from a junk dealer in Hadleigh, Suffolk, who had a mass of assorted garden furniture.

Incidentally, many of these ornaments are being reproduced today and sell at reasonable prices. It is sometimes hard to tell the difference between original and reproduction, particularly since some of the moulds used are original pieces, complete with chips and dents. If you want to collect for investment, try to get the original articles, but, if it is just for decorating the garden, there is nothing at all wrong with the reproductions.

Garden ornaments; many of these designs are being reproduced today

CORONATION DAY 1902   JUNE 26TH 1902

FRY'S
PURE SOLUBLE
BREAKFAST
COCOA
J. S. FRY & SONS, LTD.

MADE BY
FRY'S

"SAFETY" BRAND

SELECTED
STEEL PENS
BEST QUALITY.

Coronation of KING GEORGE V. AND QUEEN MARY 1911

Urillac

REGAL
LOUD TONE
NEEDLES
200   200

MENTHOLYPTUS
SNUFF

BOURNVILLE
COCOA
Cadbury

PLAYER'S
NAVY CUT.
Gold
Leaf
CIGARETTES

OXO
IN CUBES

TINS

In the nineteenth century manufacturers of foodstuffs, cigarettes, and sweets began to package their goods in tins. To make them more attractive and to create an impact at the point of sale – as modern advertizing jargon has it – they decorated these tins by means of paint, offset lithography, or transfers, for example.

Biscuit tins were particularly interesting, and as they were mass produced and well made a great many have survived, even if they have gone a little rusty on the inside. They have become collectors' items, in some cases to house other collectible articles.

A sculptor I know, who rolls his own cigarettes, keeps the tobacco and papers in a flat brass-coated tobacco tin, which he picked up a few years ago for threepence. It was the type issued to the troops in France during the First World War. Cigarette tins became more common after the war, when more and more brands were marketed.

Today, when so much money is spent on disposable packaging, which cannot be used once the contents have been consumed, one may miss the days when one could buy fifty *Passing Cloud* cigarettes in a delightful oval tin, smoke them, and then store nails or screws in the tin. Because so many people did use these tins for such purposes, you should with little difficulty find an elderly relative willing to part with one or two.

You can still buy some throat lozenges in tins, but I do not recall having seen any shaped like the diamond lozenges which were once so popular. In Victorian and Edwardian times, lozenge tins often had such features as canted corners. I also doubt whether you will be able to buy plated pins in a tin any longer. So why not collect tins of earlier times and keep in them the things they originally contained?

While looking for tins, you could also get one or two money-boxes of tin. Before the war, I remember seeing one which was shaped like a pillar-box. The coins went through the letter slit and you could only get them out by cutting open the tin.

Selection of early 20th-century tins

OTHER CONTAINERS

Over the last century or so a most engaging variety of pocket containers, such as cigarette cases, cigar cases, visiting-card cases, wallets, match holders, pill boxes, and snuff boxes, was produced. Such containers were made, often with colourful and decorative skill, in a wide range of materials, including tortoiseshell, silver, mother-of-pearl, ebony, ivory, leather, silver plate, gold, beadwork, wood, papier-mâché, and glass. This is a field in which you can build up an interesting collection quite easily and without great expense.

Silver and silver-plate containers were often engraved with initials or coats of arms. Sometimes a message or dedication was inscribed on the inside. But they are likely to be of more value if they are free from all engraving.

The card cases veneered on the outside with diamond-shaped pieces of mother-of-pearl are really not suitable for carrying about today. Nor are the beautifully lacquered papier-mâché ones, that you can still get for a few pounds. I would keep them at home on display. If you want to put your cards in a case, it would be better to use one of wood or metal.

You could also include purses and spectacle cases in your container collection. In the illustration you will see a purse made of thin steel links. I have had it for years, and it has always been known as the 'chain mail purse'. Purses were made of leather, beadwork, silver, and there were even glass ones with metal clasps and hinges. One kind of purse which many women carried in the Victorian age was the miser purse. Made in various soft materials, these purses consisted of a sausage-shaped bag with clip openings at each end, and round the middle a band of metal, which you could slide up and down so that you had an idea of how much money was left.

Spectacle cases were made of papier-mâché, leather, silver, wood, ivory, and other materials. Very often when you buy them, you find a pair of spectacles inside. The long cases often contained lorgnettes, which were a pair of eyeglasses mounted on a long silver handle.

Collection of purses, card cases, and match cases of about 1870–1890. The 'chain-mail' purse is on the right

SOUVENIRS AND COMMEMORATIVE WARE

Manufacturers have never been slow to exploit the commercial possibilities afforded by the tourist trade, or by events of national or even local interest, and souvenirs and commemorative ware offer the collector a wide and varied field.

We have already seen that the Victorians made a great deal of commemorative china. They also produced articles in glass, wood, papier-mâché, stone, metal, ivory, and many other materials. You could, however, concentrate on commemorative ware of later years, from, for example, 1900 up to the end of the Second World War. Articles of this period are not yet antique, nor will they be of much value for some time, but they are interesting sidelights on the times.

In 1935 there was a great commemorative burst for the silver jubilee of George V and Queen Mary, and when George VI and

Commemorative books and pamphlets marking various events in British history

China souvenirs from various resorts. The busts of Edward VII and Queen Alexandra commemorate King Edward's coronation in 1902

Queen Elizabeth were crowned in 1937 there were at least six 'only authentic' souvenir booklets, quite apart from the official guides. There were also pencils in red, white and blue, bearing tiny pictures of the King and Queen or the Union Jack, paper hats, flags, lapel pins, brooches, cufflinks, models of Buckingham Palace and Windsor Castle, diaries, tablemats, napkin rings, spoons, and ashtrays. Many of these items can still be found, although the articles made of paper are scarce.

Alternatively – or in addition – you could search for articles commemorating more local events, such as the centenary of a town's charter, the visit to a borough by members of the royal family, or the inauguration of an air terminal or other centre of communication.

To make collecting even easier you could simply concentrate on souvenirs from towns, seaside resorts, or country parks, either collecting the souvenirs produced by a particular town over a period of perhaps 100 years, or pursuing a theme, such as brassware, throughout the country. If you decide to collect souvenirs in brass, do not forget Dartmoor pixies and Scottish thistles.

REGIONAL WARE

Most of the collectible items we have looked at so far have not been notable for coming exclusively from one particular place, that is, they are not regional ware. There are, however, many articles which fall into this category. Regional ware is a fruitful field for collecting, and it can also provide an added interest to one's holidays.

British Isles

The countries of Britain have all produced national objects which have become internationally known. The best known of many 'exports' from Wales is the love-spoon. Welsh craftsmen have been making these wooden spoons for at least four centuries, and in recent years there has been rapid increase in the number of craftsmen producing them. They are in various forms. The most popular – and at the same time the most intricate – is the lantern and chain type. A hollow lantern shape, containing two wooden spheres, which run up and down inside, is connected by a chain of several links to a short heart-shaped spoon. In many cases the whole article was carved out of one piece of wood. It is hard to tell the age of love-

Love-spoons were formerly carved by Welsh youths and given to their sweethearts as tokens of love

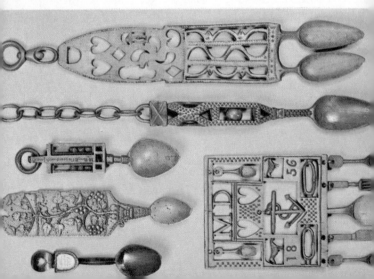

Some examples of Belleek ware

spoons, but it does not really matter, as they are equally attractive and collectible whatever their age.

Scotland has produced numerous articles that are entirely its own. Among these are fine pieces of jewellery, such as Celtic-cross brooches, silver-plate bannock racks on wooden bases (huge toast-racks for those famous flat oatmeal cakes), and dirks. Dirks are daggers with broad blades and wooden handles carved with Celtic lacework. Many were made in the nineteenth century and can be found today.

Ireland's most famous product is probably Waterford glass. In the eighteenth century a tax was imposed on glass in England. This merely prompted manufacturers to move their works over to Ireland, to such places as Cork and Waterford. As well as being much cheaper, since it was exempt from tax, the glass produced there was very well made, and it is hard even for an expert to tell the difference between the finest English and Irish glass of that period. In more recent years, however, Waterford glass has been stamped to identify it.

Another Irish product is Belleek porcelain. This is an eggshell-thin ware, which was first made in the 1860s at Belleek in

Fermanagh. Characteristic designs incorporate lattice work on the surface and small green shamrocks under the glaze.

Europe

There is a mass of collectible wares in Europe, and room here to select only a few. Some of the more attractive items of glassware to come out of the Art Nouveau and Art Deco movements, were those designed by the French artist-craftsman René Lalique. He produced moulded, pressed, and cut glass, specializing in bowls, large plates, and vases, which were all delightfully decorated in floral or foliage patterns. Some articles of Lalique ware can still be bought for five pounds or so, although many better items have fetched much greater sums.

Another collectible from France is of a very different order – old convector stoves. They were made of enamelled iron and were really quite graceful. Moreover, they can be found in good working order, and will burn wood or coal products. These interesting relics of the beginning of the century cost about forty pounds and are available in England as well as in France. There is, for example, a dealer in Camden who specializes in them.

From Spain the best-known products are some extremely fine furniture, silverwork, and tin-glazed earthenware, known

Souvenir pottery made in various Devon resorts before the First World War

Group of regional ware, including Biersteins from Germany, Dutch clogs, Spanish castanets, and an American graduation bat bearing the fraternity arms of Carnegie College, Pittsburgh

as maiolica, but these tend to be very dear. More modern collectibles include twentieth-century souvenirs. Among these are various small decorative objects of steel and cheap gold. You could hardly visit Spain without buying a miniature Toledo sword. These have been made for years, and a collection of specimens dating from, say, 1920 would be unusual.

Turning now to eastern Europe, two interesting Russian products are icons and Gardner's porcelain. Icons are representations, usually in painting, of Christ, the apostles, the saints, or other sacred personages. They go back to Byzantine times, but the sort of icons you could find quite cheaply are those made in Russia in the nineteenth century. These were painted on wood, sometimes in the form of a triptych, that is, a set of three folding panels.

Everyone has heard of icons, but few people know about Gardner's porcelain. It was made by an English craftsman who set up a factory in Moscow in the 1760s. He produced many fine, flat finish figures, of which the groups of young people or Russian peasants were particularly realistic. This ware was

19th-century icons in copper *(left)*, silver *(right)*, and enamel (below)

produced throughout the nineteenth century, and you can still buy the later pieces cheaply in Britain or Russia.

America and the rest of the world

Outside Europe, North America is an obvious source of collectibles. Quite apart from the china, glass, metalware, furniture, and cloth produced in vast quantities throughout the period we have been looking at, the Americans were first in the field with numerous mechanical and electrical inventions, many of which are mentioned in other parts of the book. An item which is peculiar to the United States is the Coca-Cola machine. Coca-Cola has been made for nearly a hundred years. In its time it has been bottled and canned, and it has been dispensed from machines fixed to or standing on bars or counters. One fountain dispenser of the 1890s was a handsome affair of porcelain. It had a lid and a recess in the lower part for the glass, which was filled with Coca-Cola supplied through a brass tap. Now quite rare, they are collected with avid enthusiasm. You are most likely to find them in the southern states.

China has been making porcelain for 2000 years. Early articles of the T'ang, and Ming dynasties, for example, fetch thousands of pounds in sales, but in the 1700s the Chinese began to make porcelain specially for export to Europe. Early articles are now both hard to find and expensive, but export ware continued to be produced in the nineteenth century, and bowls or plates can be found today for a pound or so. The best-known patterns are famille rose, which was predominantly red, and famille verte, which was mainly green.

Also from the East, Japanese colour prints have recently become a popular collector's item. In the nineteenth and early twentieth century, the Japanese reproduced many of the fine colour pictures that had been executed in earlier centuries, as far back, it is thought, as the ninth century. You can find these prints, often on coloured paper, in print and picture shops, and some cost no more than a few pounds.

Figures and masks from Benin, Nigeria, and Gold Coast, and *(third from right)* North American totem pole of carved shale

MILITARIA

I am not sure whether one can suggest collecting relics of war, without being accused of harbouring an unhealthy nostalgia for our imperial past or of being overenthusiastic about war. Taking that risk, however, I do recommend branching into militaria. Among the items that are still easy to find at low prices are badges, rank stripes, epaulettes, medal ribbons, campaign or service medals (though some are expensive), officers' belts, scabbards, holsters, caps, berets, and steel helmets. Complete uniforms, such as dress uniforms of famous regiments, SS officer uniforms, and American G.I. denim suits, are, of course, among the rarer items.

You will find several shops in London which are devoted entirely to militaria, and also some stalls in Portobello Road, Chelsea Antique Market, and the Kensington Hypermarket. They have some very fine and interesting articles, such as Hussars' plumed helmets, swords from the Waterloo campaign, medals from the Crimea, copies of staff orders, and original orders from the American War of Independence, but these are all costly, for they are very unusual. But these specialist shops may suggest ideas for collecting similar but less expensive items with, perhaps, not quite such old or celebrated connections. For example, you might start with the First World War, as its relics are still plentiful.

I suppose one cannot dismiss militaria without looking at swords and daggers. Swords ceased to be principal weapons of war (except on rare occasions) in the eighteenth century. Thereafter, they were made more for ceremonial purposes, and both army and naval officers had them. They were often very finely decorated, particularly on the pommels and hilts and, of course, the scabbards. I have seen many swords in Portobello Road marked up from about six pounds. Amongst them have been curved Turkish swords carried, if not used, in the Dardanelles campaign or in other theatres of the First World War where Turkish troops were engaged. You can also find Japanese ceremonial swords.

As for daggers, perhaps the first that comes to mind is the SS type with a swastika-emblazoned handle, or the famous curved kukri used by the Gurkhas.

Items of uniform and equipment in use during the First and Second World Wars, including tunic and cap of the Royal Horse Artillery, Imperial German field cap, steel helmet, bayonet and scabbard, and British service respirator, c. 1937

BUTTONS

Fifteen years ago few people would have thought buttons worth collecting. Then, in 1961, a collection of buttons, many of them painted with landscapes and monuments, and covered with glass, was put up for sale at Sotheby's in nearly 200 lots and fetched a total of over £6,600.

From that moment, people everywhere began to look for buttons. Before long the vast range of buttons which had been made over the centuries in glass, china, stone, mother-of-pearl, horn, ivory, pewter, copper, silver, gold, enamel, wood, painted silk, papier-mâché, and many other materials became eagerly sought after. Shops began to specialize – there is one off Oxford Street in London that deals exclusively in buttons – and in the United States a National Button Society was formed, which published its proceedings in a regular journal. Inevitably, books about buttons followed.

On the whole, except some obviously rare examples, buttons, which were generally manufactured in vast quantities, have today become over-priced, and collecting them is more expensive than it need be. But it is not too late to start.

Crested livery buttons from famous or noble households are comparatively rare, and a great deal of fun can be had in trying to build up a collection of those from well-known families, such as Bedford, Pembroke, or Bath. Alternatively, you can look for identity buttons, such as those of military regiments, government departments, railways, and shipping lines. Some hunts had – and still have – their own crested buttons.

In the United States a new aspect of advertising appeared at the beginning of the century, when advertising buttons were produced. Made of celluloid and carrying pictures and slogans exhorting people to buy various products, they were manufactured in vast quantities and can be bought in America for about a dollar or so today.

On both sides of the Atlantic buttons were also made as commemorative items. Much sought after in the United States are the buttons made to mark the advent of various railroads.

Collection of buttons showing the wide variety of materials used. On the fourth row are five crested livery buttons

19th- and early 20th-century fans *(above)* made of ostrich feathers, paper, and lace, and *(right)* of perforated sandalwood, embroidered satin, and painted paper and bamboo

FANS AND PARASOLS

A lot has been written about fans, and one would not wish to include more than an outline on this somewhat overplayed field of collecting. Fans were first used in Western Europe in the Middle Ages. Many of the more intricate ones carried concealed *poignards* or stilettos, as it was often dangerous to walk alone after nightfall or in a dark alley, especially in Renaissance Italy. Fans were of course functional, serving to keep off flies, shield one from the heat of a fire, or create a current of fresh air. Gradually, fans became an almost essential accessory for the fashionable, and no skill or expense was spared in their design and manufacture. It is beyond the scope of this book to discuss any but those of the last century or so.

Some nineteenth-century fans were made of lace, with ribs and end pieces of ivory, tortoiseshell, or mother-of-pearl. Here was a chance for the finest exponents of lace-making, like the Chantilly lace-makers of France, or those of Brussels, Nottingham, or Coggeshall in Essex, to demonstrate their skills. These fans were not often original in design, but were good copies. Some were made of paper and painted in a variety of styles; others were made of silk of different colours. You can find fans in many shops, though they are often damaged: the material has perished, the tassels are missing, and the ivory or shell is cracked.

Parasols, it is known, were used by the ancient Sumerians as long ago as 3000 BC and they have been made ever since. Our grandmothers' parasols had a lot of use, on summer walks in the park, at the races, on or near the river. They were made of lace and chiffon or muslin, with ivory or wooden shafts. It was apparently considered fashionable to have one's dress and parasol in matching material, with the result that the frame was continually being re-covered. Most of these nineteenth-century parasols have perished or only the frames remain. If you do find one with its original covering, I would not open it too often or the fabric will tear.

(left) Wedding dress of 1903, and *(right)* a Victorian riding dress, c. 1875

CLOTHES

After about a century clothes, if they last as long as that, become rather fragile. You could probably wear them now and again, but not often, and they would certainly not stand up to modern cleaning techniques. Although an enormous amount of clothing was manufactured in the second half of the last century, only a fraction remains, and in many instances the garments are in museums. Some of the costumes that have lasted have come on the open market in recent years.

By the middle of the nineteenth century, much of the colour and decoration had gone out of men's clothes, and black and white had become the predominant colours. This was largely because many men worked who fifty years earlier would have led an idle existence in or on the fringes of Regency society; clothes had become working clothes. When, in the 1830s, Disraeli rose to make his first speech in the House of Commons, his colourful clothes caused so much laughter that he had to sit down again. The late Georgian frockcoat lasted throughout the century, although it became fuller and less cut away. The top hat also lasted. It has been said that you could have worn an 1860 suit in the 1900s and no one would have noticed anything odd.

A new garment for country wear was the Norfolk jacket, a loosely belted single-breasted jacket. This was worn with knickerbockers, which in the years following the First World War were modified slightly and known as plus-fours. These hilarious garments went well with the slim, shapeless dresses of the flappers of the 1920s. I think it unlikely that you will find many nineteenth-century Norfolk jackets, but about a year ago I bought a pair of 1920s plus-fours and matching jacket for under twenty pounds.

Not surprisingly, women's dress styles changed constantly. In the mid nineteenth century, skirts were supported by very wide crinolines. Huge hats went out and were replaced by smaller bonnets. Then came the fashion for bustles and trains, which lasted fifteen years or so, until towards the end of the century dresses became simpler and more close fitting.

Victorian clothes on sale in a street market

KNOBS AND KNOCKERS

For well over two hundred years, householders have concerned themselves with the kind of doorknocker they have on the front door and with the handles and locks on the inside doors.

Knockers were made in cast iron, brass, copper, and bronze, and an enormously colourful range of designs was produced. Typical designs were of dolphins (these strange creatures were a great favourite), lions' heads, fox heads, festoons of flowers, hands, clenched or open, heads of Greek goddesses, usually with very severe expressions, urns, and in Art Nouveau times sinuous flower stems. These knockers or rappers were usually well made. It is, of course, hard to tell their age, but that splendid authority on antiques, John Bedford, says that the glorious shine of Victorian brass knockers cannot be reproduced.

Inside the house were doorknobs and handles made in an

Assortment of ceramic door sets

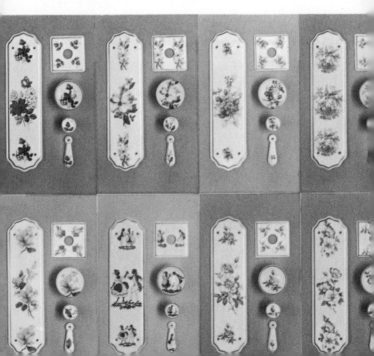

19th-century lock, knocker, and knobs in brass

equally diverse range of materials and designs. It is not unusual to find glass knobs, either round or faceted, though you
would have to pay a lot for millefiori knobs, which were made
about a century ago. Knobs were made in porcelain, pottery,
wood, ivory, jet, copper, bronze, brass, and pewter, and they
were often painted, chased, or moulded. Fingerplates were
often made to match the design of the knob, and in some houses
you find under the knob a second, smaller fingerplate, which
was protection against children with dirty fingers. Along with
the knobs and plates, bell pulls were cast to match so that you
could have a complete set for drawing room or dining room.

There is a great deal of reproduction door furniture about
today, much of it so well made that it is hard to distinguish it.
Even if you were lucky enough to know the house from which
a doorknob or fingerplate came, you could not be sure that it
had not been put in as a replacement at some time during the
house's history. Porcelain pieces, for example, crack, and after
a time they will shatter if the door is perpetually slammed; so
they have to be replaced. These difficulties should not put you
off, for door furniture can make an interesting collection.

Pencil box with Japanese decoration on the lid, letter rack inlaid with mother-of-pearl, and inlaid blotter – all in papier-mâché

PAPIER-MACHE

Possibly you may be appalled at my taste in decorative items, but I find papier-mâché work wonderful and I would like a room completely furnished with it. The Georgians and Victorians also found it agreeable, and as time went on they made almost anything decorative or functional in this material. When you consider that the range of articles in papier-mâché includes everything from beds to music racks, chairs to work-boxes, teapoys to inkwells, that nearly all these articles were decorated with fine Chinoiserie painting or very thin and skilfully inlaid mother-of-pearl, and that each piece was shaped as far as possible in the style of the time, you may understand why I like papier-mâché and regard it as a 'must' for collecting.

Papier-mâché was made of compressed layers of paper glued together, moulded and shaped while moist, and then painted and varnished when dry. It was usually painted black to set off the decoration better, but I have also seen papier-mâché articles with green and red as background colours.

Amazingly, some adventurous manufacturers made large household items and exhibited them at the Great Exhibition in 1851. The beds were, of course, iron framed, with papier-mâché dressing at each end. On the whole, heavy items of furniture were really a novelty at the time and did not catch on as well as smaller articles, which were manufactured in large numbers for many years.

I fear it is now an expensive field for would-be collectors, but you could make a start by looking for small objects, like trays, coasters, fans, letter racks, inkwells, and pen trays, which can be picked up for a few pounds each. It seems, moreover, that there are places where one can get papier-mâché repaired, so do not be put off if an article is damaged.

Papier-mâché is comparatively easy to make, and I often wonder why it has never come back into fashion as a material for household articles.

Pair of attractive papier-mâché fans

WALKING STICKS

When I was at Oxford, I always carried a walking stick. I used to collect the simpler ones with silver or plate knobs and tried to sport a different one each day of the week, but few people today use sticks, unless they are disabled and actually need them as an aid to walking. Even then, the 'medical' walking stick is a simple ash affair with no special features.

In Victorian and Edwardian days, however, most men about town carried sticks. The shafts were made of cane or of various woods, including ash, vine, teak, ebony, beech, and blackthorn, and they came in a variety of thicknesses and lengths. Some were very flexible; others were almost impossible to bend. Of course, many could not support any real weight and were, in fact, designed for show rather than use.

While the shafts are varied and interesting, it is really the heads that are the more attractive part, and what an astonishing

Selection of walking sticks, including *(third from left)* an Art Nouveau top of silver

Four more walking sticks. The right-hand top is of porcelain

variety has been made, even in the last hundred years, in silver, gold, bronze, pinchbeck, tin, pewter, ivory, glass, porcelain, mother-of-pearl, amber, horn, wood, and leather! It almost seems as if each stick was individually made with loving care and skill for a specific person.

People have collected walking sticks for a long time, and most of the more unusual ones have by now disappeared into famous collections. I seldom pass a junk-shop window, however, without noticing a stick or two. The more simple silver- or metal-headed variety usually costs about two or three pounds. You could make a start by picking a theme, such as animal heads. When you have accumulated a dozen or so, mount them on a wall; they would make an interesting display.

In our grandfathers' day, walking sticks were often made to serve two purposes. A typical dual purpose stick, which is still made today, is the sword stick. A thin steel blade attached to the head of the stick is sheathed by the shaft. Another example is the drinking stick. This has a long and extremely thin screw-capped tube, which slides down the shaft. Dual purpose sticks are not very easy to find, and if they are in reasonable condition they usually cost at least ten pounds.

RAILWAY RELICS

No psychologist has yet been able to explain why so many people are so enthusiastic about railways and all the paraphernalia associated with them. There seems to be an engine-driver or a trainspotter in everybody, and the regret for the passing of the days of steam is greater than for any other national or international object of nostalgia. There are railway societies, railway magazines, railway museums, and people get together to rescue defunct lines. They buy or rent them, repair the tracks, renovate the engines, refurbish the carriages, and run holiday or excursion services, many of which make profits. There are shops devoted to railway relics. One such shop is operated by British Rail near Euston Station.

This is a most helpful place to start collecting railway relics. You can get all kinds of things at low prices. Station signs make a good beginning. The older private railway company signs are perhaps rather rare, but even since the railways were nationalized there have been several styles of sign, and some of the earlier ones are beginning to look like strangers. Another

Some of the railway fittings on sale at British Rail's Collector's Corner at Euston Station

This invalid chair was used on railway platforms in the 1920s

item which would need a bit of room to store is an invalid carriage of the 1920s like the one in the illustration. This had poles so that station porters could pull it along the platform from the train to the ambulance.

More conventional but nonetheless fascinating, and in some cases adaptable for use in the home, are such items as lamps, washbasins, sliding bolts with 'vacant' and 'engaged' signs (I have one of these on my bathroom door), and luggage racks.

Other useful sources for the railway enthusiast are the various railway magazines and *Exchange and Mart*, which often carries advertisements for railway relics, some of which are for exchange. Alternatively, you could go to local railway depots and ask whether there are any scrap items for sale. Well-known stopping places and junctions, such as Swindon and Crewe, may have rich stocks. Remember, too, that, even though it is only in the last decade or so that the steam engine has gone out of use, anything relating to pre-diesel days is already beginning to take on the aspect of an antique.

Vintage cars can be great fun, and some, like the sporty two-seater Fiat Balilla pictured here, can still be found at surprisingly low prices

MISCELLANEOUS COLLECTIBLES

'Miscellaneous' pages of a book are invariably left to the end for those items which cannot conveniently be fitted in elsewhere. In this huge arena of inexpensive antiques, however, one could fill another hundred pages or so with articles, commonplace and unusual, which are no longer being made and are therefore of interest to the collector. Unfortunately, only a few items selected at random can be included here.

Postboxes and streetlights

A man I know collects postboxes. He has one inside the front door of his home, and the local postman pops his letters in it. This relic, the type that was bracketed to a telegraph pole, is an Edward VII box and was sold to my friend when the local post office was demolished. Pillar-boxes are of many shapes and sizes – round, square, hexagonal, or oval, with domed, gabled, or hooded tops – and you can buy them from the various post office regional depots up and down the country. See if you can get a Queen Victoria box; these are rare.

Another article which can be collected with the help of local authorities is the street lamp. Today you can buy the old four-sided shades with gabled tops as separate items from many ironwork or junk shops, but to get a complete Victorian street lamp and post will require a little more work. Some electricity board depots have them and will part with them cheaply, if only to get them off the maintenance yard. At Christmas 1972, Kingston Borough Council was selling street lamps for £7 each, with an extra charge for delivering to your door. Other council authorities are following suit. Where you would put them once you had three or four is perhaps no great problem if you live in the country. They make excellent garden lights, or, if you live in a village that has no streetlighting, you could put one over the front gate. Many of these lamps carry the arms or

A Victorian pillarbox

initials of the authority which installed them. Gas lamps are particularly interesting, as they have the levers and chains which were operated by lamplighters to turn them on and off.

Luggage

Luggage would also make a rather off-beat collection. You can find suitcases and trunks in all sorts of places for paltry sums. They are frequently turned out and thrown away when people move house; they are invariably found in attics or cellars when houses are demolished. Suitcases with expanding locks and hinges were already being made half a century ago. The covering and straps were in fine-quality leather, and although the cases were very heavy they lasted for years. In Victorian times suitcases were often squarer in shape, deeper, and altogether more like a trunk. They came in many sizes. Some were small enough to be carried in one hand by means of a single handle near the lock. The larger ones were sometimes reinforced with wooden slats on the lid and round the sides. The lids might be domed, bowed, or flat. The locks and hinges were brassy and ornate, and gave an air of security.

When our grandparents went picnicking on summer Sundays, they did so in style. Their picnic baskets and hampers were most elaborate, and are now very desirable as collectors' pieces. Some months ago I bought for twenty pounds a fine leather box containing a square metal pot with spout, a spirit stove, a container for methylated spirits, a square milk bottle with metal cap, square canisters for sugar, jam, and tea or coffee, and a pair of very lightweight porcelain cups and saucers in an orange, red and white pattern. It was made in Constantinople just before the First World War, probably as a souvenir piece for visitors to take home. I have also seen, for very much less, individual utensil sets. One, in a cylindrical leather case about 8 inches high and 3 inches in diameter, contained a conical silver-plate beaker, inside which was a leather roll containing a cylinder in polished metal, and a knife, fork and spoon. The cutlery had bone handles, and each piece folded in half like a penknife. The knife and spoon had attach-

Some of the hampers, picnic baskets, and travelling kits which could be bought at the Army and Navy Stores in 1907

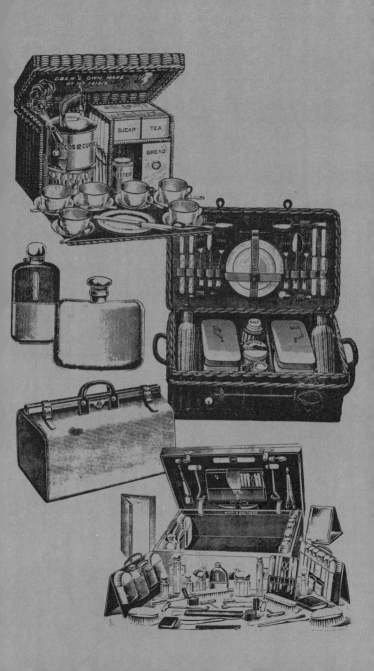

ments in the handle: a corkscrew in one, and a pair of tweezers in the other. The cylinder was in three parts, which screwed together; the first section was a saltcellar, the second a pepper-pot, and the third container was for mustard.

Stamps and coins

No general book on collecting would, I suppose, be complete without mention of stamps and coins, those two very popular fields which most people seem to embark on in childhood. Stamps are unique. Intrinsically, they are absolutely worthless, and yet, because of a quirk in their printing or design, some can be worth thousands. Obviously, if you are limited to in-expensive antiques, you are not going to be able to compete in the area of rare issues. Perhaps the best way to start is to make thematic collections. Choose a subject – railways, for example – and build up a sheet or two of stamps from the countries which have commemorated or celebrated railways in some way. During the last decades of the nineteenth century, the United States printed several railway stamps, and this theme has also figured on the stamps of many other countries, including the Balkan States, Russia, and China.

Most towns and cities have at least one stamp shop, and you

Parts of various stamp collections built up according to subject or nationality

Coins from many countries, dating from Roman times to the present day. The banknotes were issued in France during the First World War

can also buy stamps through specialist magazines. Prices vary of course, but a useful guide is the Stanley Gibbons catalogue, which comes out in a new edition every year.

In some respects, coins are not very different. On the whole their metal value is extremely small, unless they are gold or silver. Their value depends on other factors, such as rarity, age, and condition. Again, there are numerous coin dealers, and on many of the stalls in antique markets, such as those in Chelsea and Oxford Street, you will find trays of assorted coins. You could start by collecting Roman coins. The Romans were in Britain for 400 years, and a great many of their coins have been unearthed. Most of them carried portraits of the emperors, and this can be helpful in dating them if you have a list of the emperors from Augustus (27 BC–AD 14) to Honorius (AD 395–423). A coin of Hadrian (AD 117–138), who built the wall in Northumberland and Cumberland, would cost about £5. A Charles II silver crown could cost as little as £1.25, but this would be because it was badly damaged in some way; the condition of a coin is very important in valuing it.

ART NOUVEAU

We have already seen that towards the end of the nineteenth century there was a revolt against the current heavy sumptuous and often vulgar architecture, decoration, and furnishings. In Britain the leaders of this revolt were William Morris and his artist-craftsmen, Aubrey Beardsley, the artist who specialized in book illustration, C. R. Ashbee, the architect who greatly influenced jewellery designs, and C. R. MacIntosh, the Scottish architect who designed furniture. In France Gallé, the glassmaker, was a leading light, and in the U.S.A. Tiffany, the owner of a large American store, encouraged new ideas and often provided the finance for them.

It is now very fashionable to collect Art Nouveau, and much of it is expensive. A real Tiffany lamp, for example, will be beyond the means of many, but the movement was all-pervading, and many of the more ordinary household articles have survived. Among the items to look for are tiles. Many were designed by Morris or by his friend William de Morgan, and these were decorated with colourful floral patterns, exotic birds, or sinuous plants. In large quantities they will be costly, as buyers want them for fireplace surrounds, but singles and pairs can still be bought for under a pound. Mounted in simple iron frames, they make excellent pictures.

Silver and silver plate received the new treatment. Teaspoons, for example, are easily recognizable, for their bowls are pointed, and the handles are spidery or twisted, sometimes with a stone inset among the curves at the end. Copper was a material favoured by the craftsmen, and mirrors, candlesticks, and other articles of beaten copper contained willowy flower-stem motifs. The same sinuous designs also recur on the pottery of the period.

If you are interested in Art Nouveau, visit the Church at Great Warley, Essex, where the stained glass, woodcarving, embroidery, metalwork, and stonework are all in this exciting and distinctive style.

Art Nouveau interior with occasional table inlaid with floral and butterfly patterns in various woods, rosewood chair with semi-cabriole legs and carved back, and glass vase, c. 1898

Ornamental items in the Art Deco style

ART DECO

If you consider Art Nouveau weird, unpleasant, or decadent, what, I wonder, would you think of its successor, Art Deco? This amazing decorative style burst upon Western Europe and America in the second decade of this century, reaching its height in the 1920s. It came in with southern states jazz, with the flappers, and with the drawing-room comedies of Noel Coward and others, and it gave more permanent expression to that curious time when mankind, in the West at all events, was riding high for a fall – which came when Wall Street crashed in 1929.

The most obtrusive features of Art Deco were the glaring colours, the predominance of shiny, gleaming, sunny bright motifs, and the impractical designs and materials. It was the age of people like Isadora Duncan, and Art Deco enthusiasts craved for ivory, porcelain, or metal figures of contemporary dancers. Grotesque as some of these statuettes are, they are now quite expensive.

Like any other style, Art Deco had its pioneering heroes, and some of them are still alive. One was Russian-born Erté, who fled to the West during the 1917 Revolution and set up as a dress designer. His designs were an enormous success in the twenties, as they captured the frivolity of the young people who danced the black bottom or the Charleston all night long and smoked cigarettes through extremely long holders. Erté's work also extended into the fields of furniture, jewellery, and art. He produced a variety of bizarre lithographs, which are now fetching high prices.

The wild decorative ideas of the decade were reflected in the more mundane domestic ware which 'smart' people bought for their gaudily wallpapered homes. A typical Art Deco tea-service, which you might find quite cheaply, was the cube-shaped set. The saucers and plates were square, and the cups and teapot were cube shaped. Other tea-services were more conventional in shape, but were decorated with stark designs painted in bright colours. Those by Clarice Cliffe of the Newport Pottery were very popular.

More examples of Art Deco, now eagerly sought by collectors

(above and right) Assortment of 20th-century kitsch. Will these be among the collector's items of the future?

KITSCH

Have you heard of kitsch? It is a German word used to describe decorative articles which are really vulgar and taste-less by any standards. The Oxford definition of kitsch is 'worthless pretentiousness in (esp. dramatic) art', and if this is too vague an example or two may help to illustrate its meaning.

One example of kitsch is model fruit. In some houses you used to see a fruit bowl piled up with apples, pears, bananas, and grapes, all of which looked very tempting – until you touched them! They were made of glazed pottery or, in later years, plastic. A development of this idea was the plastic flower. In the early 1960s dozens of different flowers were being copied in plastic. They were sold in shops, given away with washing powder, and some manufacturers even made contracts with public houses and the like to supply them with a different plastic flower arrangement every month.

Pottery flying ducks also come under the heading of kitsch. Sold in sets of three or four, graded in size, but in all other respects completely identical, they were usually to be seen winging their way across a wall or chimneybreast. Judging by the number of times they are mentioned in contemporary British plays and television scripts, flying ducks have now passed into the folklore of the British lower middle class.

Kitsch was by no means limited to Britain, nor indeed was it really first evident here. Take, for instance, some of the posters produced in Germany, Italy, and Belgium between the wars. Created by commercial designers with artistic pretensions, they are classic examples of kitsch, and in fact kitsch is perhaps best described as decoration purporting to be art. But in saying this one has to be careful not to offend. There will always be someone who will defend even the gawky poster as a work of art. Furthermore, items widely regarded as kitsch are fetching high prices. In fact, it can be as profitable catering for people's bad taste as for their good. Had the word been coined by the Victorians, I am quite sure many of the articles they liked, such as fairings, would have ranked as kitsch.

(above and right) Some examples of elegant, well-made 20th-century reproductions of earlier styles

POTENTIAL ANTIQUES

Having looked at some ideas for buying inexpensive items which are likely to increase in value quickly, it may be helpful to consider some contemporary articles to see what kind of object is likely to become a collector's piece in the future. Any kind of list covering such an enormous field would be incomplete because there are so many things in other parts of the world that we in Europe and North America have never even thought of. Add to that the question of individual likes and dislikes, and you can see that general guide lines are the best one can provide.

One need take only a brief look at the history of collecting to see that, next to buying original works of art or antiques, collectors have bought good reproductions. Over the past two centuries, each era, including the present one, has had its share of craftsmen and manufacturers who have reproduced articles of an earlier age. They have done so because of their own preference for the older styles and also because there has been a demand for them.

Thinking of the future, then, you could make a start by accumulating reproductions. If you cannot have an original set of six Regency rope-back Trafalgar chairs for the dining room, then why not have a set of copies? They are often as well made as the originals and they fulfil exactly the same function. Many firms make reproduction eighteenth-century or Regency chairs, occasional tables, and dining tables, and really the only way to judge is to satisfy yourself that you like the way the work has been done. Bear in mind, however, that there are a lot of pieces which, although made in the correct style, are twentieth-century modifications. For example, coffee tables and drinks tables were virtually unknown in Georgian times.

Most of the well-known makes of porcelain and pottery are still being produced, and you could profitably collect items

by Wedgwood, Derby, Worcester, Doulton, Minton, Copeland, Dresden, Sèvres, and Limoges. These firms, like many others, are still producing some of their traditional designs and patterns. In 1958 I was given as a wedding present a charming little jug and bowl made by the Royal Crown Derby Porcelain Company. They were brand new but they were reproductions of a style the firm used to make in the early nineteenth century.

As for glass, several firms are now making fine copies of eighteenth-century wineglasses, rummers, bowls, and jugs.

You may find that the best reproductions are made by country firms and craftsmen, and a list of these can be obtained from the Council for Small Industries in Rural Areas, 35 Camp Road, London SW19, which publishes a booklet every year containing the names of about 1000 craftsmen of all skills.

Various firms are making copies of many other functional and decorative articles used in earlier ages. I recently saw a small reproduction terrestrial globe on a stand made of wood. It is possible that in years to come this may be sought by collectors. Similarly, a Japanese cigarette-lighter in the form of a lady's pistol of the nineteenth century, which ignites when you pull the trigger, may become an interesting relic.

Mention of cigarette lighters leads me to suggest these as articles to collect. They have been made for the last half-century or so, and have come in some interesting and unusual guises. For example, why not look for porcelain dice in red or blue with white dots, or silver-plate table lighters shaped like Queen Anne or Georgian teapots or urns.

Many people dislike modern dining room furniture, but one or two of the larger manufacturers are producing some quite pleasant individual styles, which are well made. A good example is the G-Plan suite illustrated on page 147, which I believe may well be of interest to collectors in the next century. So – one final suggestion – if you are thinking of ditching your G-Plan and replacing it with a reproduction Georgian suite, rather than sell the G-Plan (for it will not fetch much on the second-hand market today), keep it in the garage – and wait.

'Fresco' dining room furniture by G-Plan – an attractive and distinctive style which may be sought after in the future

HOW TO BUY AND WHERE

It seems almost an impertinence to advise anyone on how to go into a shop and buy an inexpensive relic of the past. But I have had a shop and I have known a great many dealers. Most adopt a variety of guises, whether the object for sale is valuable or not. Indeed, it seems that after a while some dealers reach the stage when the value, usefulness, or elegance of a piece is of no consideration. Some leave their goods unpriced.

Model cars attract young buyers at an open-air sale. Prices can be deceptively high

This enables them to assess you, the prospective buyer, and fix a price on the spot. Beware of one of the oldest, most stupid, and most dishonest chestnuts: 'It's yours for £5. I gave £4.50 and I had to bring it here, so there's nothing in it for me.' If you think £5 is reasonable, or if you feel you can afford it, then offer the dealer £4.50 and see if he will accept. If he does not and you still want the article, then pay the asking price. But I would always try to bargain with any dealer, no matter how smart the shop or how costly the goods on display.

There is another type of dealer, who will try to blind you with knowledge. His article of furniture will always be the one which has the unusual marquetry in holly wood, his willow pattern meat-plate will always be one with thirty-two apples on the tree, instead of the more usual thirty-four, or his copper ale-measures will be genuine mid eighteenth century. This same 'expertise' is now being applied even to the kind of inexpensive articles we have been looking at in this volume.

With this background, you should feel happy about going into any shop. If you are not, then try the salesrooms. Country-house sales or sales in very small towns are more productive for the collector of inexpensive items than the larger and better-known salesrooms. In a country-house sale, the object is to auction off everything, and this is where you may get your chance. Auction rooms in small towns usually have difficulty in filling 300 lots, which is the size of sale to attract buyers, and so they accept less expensive items. Those that do not quite often have special sales for cheaper goods, usually described as *Furniture and Household Items*, or something similar.

Jumble sales, sales of work, autumn, Christmas, and spring fairs can often produce unexpected bargains. After all, many people will give to local sales articles which they would refuse to sell to an unknown dealer who came knocking on their door.

More serious collectors should scan the pages of *Exchange and Mart*, local papers, and the various trade magazines. For those who want to get more deeply involved in a particular field, here is a list of specialist collectors' societies and associations in Britain and America:

Antique Collectors' Club, Woodbridge, Suffolk

Antique Bottle Collectors' Association, PO Box 467, Sacramento, California 95802

(above and right) Country antique shop in the United States, with a wide and interesting variety of goods on display

National Button Society, 7940 Montgomery Avenue, Elkins Park, Philadelphia, Pennsylvania 19117

Society of Caddy Spoon Collectors, 43 Pine Avenue, Gravesend, Kent

English Ceramic Circle, 23 Cliveden Place, London SW1

Cigarette Card Society, Cambridge House, 34 Wellesley Road, London W4

City of London Phonograph and Gramophone Society, 148 Nether Street, West Finchley, London N3

Music Box Society, 14 Elmwood Road, London W4

Newspaper Collectors' Club, 8 Monks Avenue, New Barnet, Hertfordshire

Paperweight Collectors' Association, 47 Windsor Road, Scarsdale, New York

Pewter Society, The Wold, 12 Stratford Crescent, Cringleford, Norwich

Postcard Club of Great Britain, 34 Harper House, St James' Crescent, London SW9

Better Postcard Collectors' Club, 318 Roosevelt Avenue, Folshom, Pennsylvania 19033

Stevengraph Collectors' Association, Daisy Lane, Irvington, New York

Antique Toy Collectors' Club, 8110 Frankford Avenue, Philadelphia 10533

GLOSSARY

Bracket foot, a foot which supports a piece of furniture, such as a chest of drawers, wardrobe, cupboard, or coffer, and is fitted to the underframe at both sides of the corner. The front bracket is usually shaped or cut out

Bun foot, a squashed ball foot, found on 17th- and 18th-century cabinets and chests, and again on Victorian large chests

Cabriole leg, a leg, usually on tables and chairs, which tapers downwards, at first along an outward and then along an inward curve, and terminates in a decorated foot

Cameo, a stone or shell carved in relief in a way which brings out the contrast between the different colours of the material used. The most usual but not the only colours are white and rust, the figure being white and the background rust

Canting, flattening of a corner of a square or rectangular section of wood. Also known as chamfering or bevelling

Caryatid, a sculptured figure of a woman used as a support on a piece of furniture

Cast iron, ironwork which is produced by pouring molten iron into a pre-shaped mould

Ceramics, a generic term for porcelain, pottery, terracotta, etc.

Chinoiserie, decorative artwork which has Chinese characteristics, such as fretwork and pagodas

Ebonized, (of wood) stained to look like ebony, which is a black or very dark brown tropical wood found in Ceylon and India

Electrolysis, the process of breaking down chemical compounds by passing an electric current through them in solution. By this process, thin layers of metal can be deposited on other metals for protective or decorative purposes. It is the basis of electroplating with silver

Lacquering, the process of applying several layers of paint and special varnish to produce a decorated surface

Lithography, a printing process devised in Germany at the end of the eighteenth century on the principle that oil and water do not mix. The image is drawn with a special crayon on a flat surface (originally of limestone, now more commonly of aluminium or zinc), over which water is then passed. When smeared with greasy ink only the crayoned area will accept it, and the image can be printed in the normal way

Mosaic, a decoration, usually on walls, floors, or ceilings, made by cementing together small pieces of coloured stone or glass to form a pattern or picture

Moulding, a member shaped to provide decorative effect, such as that used to enclose panels on a cupboard or a shaped edge of a table, pediment, or cornice, etc.

Ogee, a double curve, the upper part being convex and the lower concave, often applied to wooden bracket feet

Mosaic floor at Fishbourne Roman Palace

Oleograph, a reproduction of a painting in oils, in which the colours of the original were copied by colour lithography

Parian ware, a mixture of porcelain and glass used in imitation of marble. Introduced in the 1840s, it was very easy to model and was most popularly used for statuary

Pediment, a triangular structure on the top of certain items of furniture, such as longcase clocks

Pilaster, a rectangular column, particularly one which forms an abutment on a wall or panel

Pinchbeck, an alloy of zinc and copper used in imitation of gold

Reeding, a form of wood decoration of convex mouldings adjacent in rows, either as surfacing for a turned leg or as ornament on a flat surface

Rococo, typified by light gay asymmetrical designs, such as those which dominated European architecture, decoration, and furniture in the first half of the 18th century

Serpentine, a form of shaping to fronts or surface edges of certain pieces of furniture, in which the ends curve inwards to meet the centre section, which curves outwards

Spelter, zinc, especially impure zinc, used in the 19th century for figures and often coloured to look like bronze

Transfer, a decorative pattern or picture engraved on a copper plate and applied to porcelain, pottery, enamel, etc., by means of paper tissues. In the 19th century transfer printing on ceramics was done before or after glazing

Veneer, a thin layer of wood, originally cut by hand, but by machine after the beginning of the 19th century, used to surface or decorate the carcase of a piece of furniture

Wrought iron, iron which is worked into shape by heating, hammering, and chilling

Louis XV commode with typical rococo decoration

BOOKS TO READ

What's New That's Old? by John Mebane. A. S. Barnes, New York, 1969.

The World of Antiques by Plantagenet Somerset Fry. Hamlyn, London, 1970.

Looking in Junk Shops by John Bedford. Macdonald, London, 1961.

More Looking in Junk Shops by John Bedford. Macdonald, London, 1962.

The Victoriana Collector's Handbook by C. Platten Woodhouse. Bell, London, 1970.

The World of Victoriana by James Norbury. Hamlyn, London, 1972.

The Victorian Scene by Nicolas Bentley. Spring Books, London, 1968.

Victoriana by Jüri Gabriel. Hamlyn, London, 1969.

Buying Antiques: General Guide by A. W. Coysh and John King. David & Charles, London, 1970.

Complete Antiques Price List by Ralph and Terry Kovel. Crown, New York, 1971.

More Small Decorative Antiques by Therle Hughes. Lutterworth Press, London, 1962.

Antique China and Glass under Five Pounds by Geoffrey Godden. Barker, London, 1966.

Collecting Cheap China and Glass by Guy Richard Williams. Corgi, London, 1969.

Bristol and Other Coloured Glass by John Bedford. Cassell, London, 1964.

The Picture Postcard and Its Origins by Frank Staff. Lutterworth Press, London, 1966.

Collecting Cigarette Cards by D. Bagnall. Arco, London, 1965.

History of Valentines by R. W. Lee. Batsford, London, 1953.

Victorian Sheet Music Covers by Ronald Pearsall. David & Charles, London, 1972.

Stevengraphs and Other Victorian Silk Pictures by Geoffrey Godden. Barrie & Jenkins, London, 1971.

Collecting Copper and Brass by Geoffrey Wills. Mayflower, London, 1970.

Tunbridge and Scottish Souvenir Woodware by Edward and Eva Pinto. Bell, London, 1970.

World of Toys by Robert Cluff. Hamlyn, London, 1969.

Art Nouveau by Martin Battersby. Hamlyn, London, 1969.

Art Deco by Bevis Hillier. Studio Vista, London, 1968.

A Guide to the Collection of Tiles. H.M.S.O., London, 1960.

What wood is that? by Herbert Edlin. Thames & Hudson, London, 1969.

ACKNOWLEDGEMENTS

Photographs are reproduced by courtesy of the following:
Athena Reproductions 143; Wm. Bartlett & Son Ltd, High
Wycombe 144, 145; British Publishing Corporation 11, 40,
54, 69, 70, 88, 89, 92, 93, 111, 126, 127, 128, 129; Collector's
Guide 53, 119; Cooper-Bridgeman Library 24, 104; David &
Charles 135; Eric Englefield 150, 151; G-Plan Gallery 147;
Hamlyn Group Picture Library 41, 57, 96, 123, 139; Keates Ltd,
Stoke on Trent 124; Motor Magazine 132, 148; Observer/
Transworld 133; Syndication International 44, 45; Wallace
Collection, London 154; Welsh Folk Museum, Cardiff 110

The publishers are grateful to the following for lending articles
to be photographed:
Almost Antique, Ealing 112; Arts d'Diane, Isleworth 5; Brian
Catley & John Sparrow, Barrett Street Antique Market,
London 43, 52, 140; Collector's Corner, Euston Station 130,
131; Crowther of Syon Lodge Ltd, Isleworth 102, 103;
Ealing Antiques 9, 16, 19, 36, 48, 85, 120; Imperial War
Museum, London 117; John Jenkins, Barrett Street Antique
Market 34, 80; Gillian Kean, Barrett Street Antique Market 81;
Kingston Antiques 30; Mansell Collection, London 59, 61,
63, 65, 108; Arthur Middleton, Barrett Street Antique Market
52, 55, 71, 80, 81, 86, 90, 95, 125; Norman Mitchell Ltd,
Feltham 142, 143; Paul New, Barrett Street Antique Market
34, 43, 68; Phelps Ltd, Twickenham 6, 7, 8, 15, 17, 18, 22,
23, 25, 26, 27, 28, 29; Piano Museum, Brentford 75, 76;
Rainbow Colour Ltd 83; Sanderson's 58; Science Museum,
London 78, 79; Paul Seidler, Barrett Street Antique Market 86;
Rita Smythe, Barrett Street Antique Market 34, 52, 71, 90;
Sussex Archaeological Trust 153

And to the following for allowing items from their collections
to be photographed:
Lorna Bellars; Mr and Mrs W. A. Brott; Mr and Mrs Plantagenet
Somerset Fry; Tom Graves; Gaby Goldscheider; E. D. Hard-
castle; John Howard; Pat Jenkins; Leigh Jones; Mary Lindsay;
W. D. Nicholson; Mary Orr; Kate Reddick; Michael Tregenza;
Deborah Trenerry

INDEX

Page numbers in bold type refer to illustrations

SOME OTHER TITLES IN THIS SERIES

- Arts
- Domestic Animals and Pets
- Domestic Science
- Gardening
- General Information
- History and Mythology
- Natural History
- Popular Science

Arts
Antique Furniture/Architecture/Clocks and Watches/Glass for Collectors/Jewellery/Musical Instruments/Porcelain/Pottery/Victoriana

Domestic Animals and Pets
Budgerigars/Cats/Dog Care/Dogs/Horses and Ponies/Pet Birds/Pets for Children/Tropical Freshwater Aquaria/Tropical Marine Aquaria

Domestic Science
Flower Arranging

Gardening
Chrysanthemums/Garden Flowers/Garden Shrubs/House Plants/Plants for Small Gardens/Roses

General Information
Aircraft/Arms and Armour/Coins and Medals/Flags/Fortune Telling/Freshwater Fishing/Guns/Military Uniforms/Motor Boats and Boating/National Costumes of the World/Orders and Decorations/Rockets and Missiles/Sailing/Sailing Ships and Sailing Craft/Sea Fishing/Trains/Veteran and Vintage Cars/Warships

History and Mythology
Age of Shakespeare/Archaeology/Discovery of: Africa/The American West/Australia/Japan/North America/South America/Great Land Battles/Great Naval Battles/Myths and Legends of: Africa/Ancient Egypt/Ancient Greece/Ancient Rome/India/The South Seas/Witchcraft and Black Magic

Natural History
The Animal Kingdom/Animals of Australia and New Zealand/Animals of Southern Asia/Bird Behaviour/Birds of Prey/Butterflies/Evolution of Life/Fishes of the world/Fossil Man/A Guide to the Seashore/Life in the Sea/Mammals of the world/Monkeys and Apes/Natural History Collecting/The Plant Kingdom/Prehistoric Animals/Seabirds/Seashells/Snakes of the world/Trees of the world/Tropical Birds/Wild Cats

Popular Science
Astronomy/Atomic Energy/Chemistry/Computers at Work/The Earth/Electricity/Electronics/Exploring the Planets/Heredity The Human Body/Mathematics/Microscopes and Microscopic Life/Physics/Undersea Exploration/The Weather Guide